Neville (

The Wish Fulfilled

Compiled and Edited

By
David Allen

Includes Lesson 2 from Neville's 1948 Classroom Lessons "Assumptions Harden Into Fact"

Printed in the United States of America

First Paperback Edition, August 2020

ISBN: 978-0-9995435-9-7

Introduction

No one has ever revealed to mankind the truth of how our minds (conscious and subconscious) work quite like Neville Goddard. Throughout his books and lectures Neville gave several examples of Imagining The Wish Fulfilled, Assuming The Wish Fulfilled, Feeling The Wish Fulfilled. Let me note here: What he meant by that is to BELIEVE that your wish is fulfilled. This should be abundantly clear to anyone who has understood Neville's teachings.

This book was compiled to capture these teachings in one book for the purpose of giving the reader a clearer and more concentrated look at what Neville was conveying about assuming the wish fulfilled.

In his words...

"Prayer is not so much what you ask for, as how you prepare for its reception.

"Whatsoever things ye desire, when ye pray believe that you have received them, and ye shall have them."

The only condition required is that you believe that your prayers are already realized. Your prayer must be answered if you assume the feeling that would be yours were you already in possession of your objective. The moment you accept the wish as an accomplished fact, the subconscious finds means for its realization. To pray successfully then, you must yield to the wish, that is, feel the wish fulfilled." - Neville Goddard

In order to better understand what Neville meant by "Feeling The Wish Fulfilled" it will be helpful for the reader to know that he meant to BELIEVE that your desire is an already accomplished fact in your life. In other words, your Wish Is Already Fulfilled as far as you are concerned. From the point of first identifying your wish, you simply speak (think, write, type, believe) FROM the Wish Fulfilled, not OF having to do anything other than that. Once you have spoken it into existence, which is what gives it form in your consciousness, the works are done. There is nothing more to do than to live from that consciousness, that you have your desire, that it is done. Rather than trying to capture the feeling in some mystical manner, you SIMPLY believe that your wish is already fulfilled. The feeling happens as a result of this act. The feeling is the assent of the subconscious once it has accepted your words as your truth, in other words, your belief.

Another way of looking at it is, you are Believing It True. You are creating your reality by what you believe to be true. Imagination, not facts, create your reality. You have always done this, now that you know how it works, you can do it consciously. To be aware of this is to be awakened to the truth.

Note: Throughout Neville's teachings he used several words that may be better understood as BELIEF. The words he used may work for many. But belief, being a synonym of those words made it clearer for me. To assume that your wish is fulfilled is to believe that it is fulfilled. To feel that your wish is fulfilled is to believe that it is fulfilled. Once you have understood this it will become clearer as you read it in Neville's own words.

If this does not work for all, then stick with what works for you. My experience has been that it does work for many. This is why I am sharing this information, for those that it may help and not those who may be set in their ways.

David Allen

The Wish Fulfilled

The feeling of the wish fulfilled, if assumed and sustained, must objectify the state that would have created it.

This law explains why

"Faith is the substance of things hoped for, the evidence of things not seen"

and why

"He calleth things that are not seen as though they were and things that were not seen become seen."

Assume the feeling of your wish fulfilled and continue feeling that it is fulfilled until that which you feel objectifies itself.

The Wish Fulfilled

Prayer . . the art of believing what is denied by the senses . . deals almost entirely with the subconscious. Through prayer, the subconscious is suggested, into acceptance of the wish fulfilled, and, reasoning deductively, logically unfolds it to its legitimate end.

The Wish Fulfilled

The subconscious mind is the universal conductor which the operator modifies with his thoughts and feelings. Visible states are either the vibratory effects of subconscious vibrations within you or they are vibratory causes of the corresponding vibrations within you. A disciplined man never permits them to be causes unless they awaken in him the desirable states of consciousness.

With knowledge of the law of reversibility, the disciplined man transforms his world by imagining and feeling only what is lovely and of good report. The beautiful idea he awakens within himself shall not fail to arouse its affinity in others.

He knows the savior of the world is not a man but the manifestation that would save.

The sick man's savior is health, the hungry man's is food, the thirsty man's savior is water. He walks in the company of the savior, by assuming the feeling of his wish fulfilled.

The Wish Fulfilled

The spiritual man speaks to the natural man through the language of desire. The key to progress in life and to the fulfillment of dreams lies in ready obedience to its voice. Unhesitating obedience to its voice is an immediate assumption of the wish fulfilled. To desire a state is to have it.

As Pascal has said,

"You would not have sought me had you not already found me."

Man, by assuming the feeling of his wish fulfilled, and then living and acting on this conviction, alters the future in harmony with his assumption.

Assumptions awaken what they affirm. As soon as man assumes the feeling of his wish fulfilled, his four-dimensional self finds ways for the attainment of this end, discovers methods for its realization.

I know of no clearer definition of the means by which we realize our desires than to experience in imagination what we would experience in the flesh were we to achieve our goal.

The Wish Fulfilled

A most effective way to embody a desire is to assume the feeling of the wish fulfilled and then, in a relaxed and sleepy state, repeat over and over again, like a lullaby, any short phrase which implies fulfillment of our desire, such as "Thank you" as though we addressed a higher power for having done it for us.

If, however, we seek a conscious projection into a dimensionally larger world, then we must keep the action going right up until sleep ensues.

Experience in imagination, with all the distinctness of reality, what would be experienced in the flesh were you to achieve your goal; and you shall, in time, meet it in the flesh as you met it in your imagination.

The Wish Fulfilled

We call things by wishing and assuming the feeling of our wish fulfilled. Unlike the world of three dimensions where there is an interval between our assumption and its fulfillment, in the dimensionally larger world there is an immediate realization of our assumption. The external reality instantly mirrors our assumption.

Here there is no need to wait four months till harvest. We look again as though we saw, and lo and behold, the fields are already white to harvest.

In this dimensionally larger world

"Ye shall not need to fight: set yourselves, stand ye still, and see the salvation of the Lord with you."

And because that greater world is slowly passing through our three-dimensional world, we can by the power of imagination mold our world in harmony with our desire. Look as though you saw, listen as though you heard; stretch forth your imaginary hand as though you touched . . and your assumptions will harden into facts.

The Wish Fulfilled

The subconscious accepts as true that which you feel as true, and because creation is the result of subconscious impressions, you, by your feeling, determine creation. You are already that which you want to be, and your refusal to believe this is the only reason you do not see it.

To seek on the outside for that which you do not feel you are, is to seek in vain, for we never find that which we want; we find only that which we are.

In short, you express and have only that which you are conscious of being or possessing.

"To him that hath it is given."

Denying the evidence of the senses and appropriating the feeling of the wish fulfilled is the way to the realization of your desire.

Mastery of self-control of your thoughts and feelings is your highest achievement.

The Wish Fulfilled

Nothing stops you from realizing your objective save your failure to feel that you are already that which you wish to be, or that you are already in possession of the thing sought.

Your subconscious gives form to your desires only when you feel your wish fulfilled.

The Wish Fulfilled

"As in heaven, so on earth."

As in the subconscious, so on earth. Whatever you have in consciousness as you go to sleep is the measure of your expression in the waking two-thirds of your life on earth. Nothing stops you from realizing your objective save your failure to feel that you are already that which you wish to be, or that you are already in possession of the thing sought.

Your subconscious gives form to your desires only when you feel your wish fulfilled.

The unconsciousness of sleep is the normal state of the subconscious. Because all things come from within yourself, and your conception of yourself determines that which comes, you should always feel the wish fulfilled before you drop off to sleep. You never draw out of the deep of yourself that which you want; you always draw that which you are, and you are that which you feel yourself to be as well as that which you feel as true of others.

To be realized, then, the wish must be resolved into the feeling of being or having or witnessing the state sought. This is accomplished by assuming the feeling of the wish fulfilled. The feeling which comes in response to the question

"How would I feel were my wish realized?"

The Wish Fulfilled

Realization of your wish is accomplished by assuming the feeling of the wish fulfilled. You cannot fail unless you fail to convince yourself of the reality of your wish.

A change of belief is confirmed by a change of expression.

The Wish Fulfilled

Man awake is under compulsion to express his subconscious impressions. If in the past he unwisely impressed himself, then let him begin to change his thought and feeling, for only as he does so will he change his world.

Do not waste one moment in regret, for to think feelingly of the mistakes of the past is to reinfect yourself.

"Let the dead bury the dead."

Turn from appearances and assume the feeling that would be yours were you already the one you wish to be.

Feeling a state produces that state. The part you play on the world's stage is determined by your conception of yourself. By feeling your wish fulfilled and quietly relaxing into sleep, you cast yourself in a star role to be played on earth tomorrow, and, while asleep, you are rehearsed and instructed in your part.

The acceptance of the end automatically wills the means of realization. Make no mistake about this.

The Wish Fulfilled

If, as you prepare for sleep, you do not consciously feel yourself into the state of the answered wish, then you will take with you into the chamber of her who conceived you the sum total of the reactions and feelings of the waking day; and while asleep, you will be instructed in the manner in which they will be expressed tomorrow.

You will rise believing that you are a free agent, not realizing that every action and event of the day is predetermined by your concept of self as you fell asleep.

Your only freedom, then, is your freedom of reaction. You are free to choose how you feel and react to the day's drama, but the drama . . the actions, events and circumstances of the day . . have already been determined.

Unless you consciously and purposely define the attitude of mind with which you go to sleep, you unconsciously go to sleep in the composite attitude of mind made up of all feelings and reactions of the day.

The Wish Fulfilled

"Except a corn of wheat fall into the ground and die, it abideth alone; but if it die, it bringeth forth much fruit."

Your conception of yourself as you fall asleep is the seed you drop into the ground of the subconscious. Dropping off to sleep feeling satisfied and happy compels conditions and events to appear in your world which confirm these attitudes of mind.

Sleep is the door into heaven.

What you take in as a feeling you bring out as a condition, action, or object in space. So sleep in the feeling of the wish fulfilled.

"As in consciousness, so on earth."

The Wish Fulfilled

Prayer is not so much what you ask for, as how you prepare for its reception.

"Whatsoever things ye desire, when ye pray believe

that you have received them, and ye shall have them."

The only condition required is that you believe that your prayers are already realized.

Your prayer must be answered if you assume the feeling that would be yours were you already in possession of your objective. The moment you accept the wish as an accomplished fact, the subconscious finds means for its realization.

To pray successfully then, you must yield to the wish, that is, feel the wish fulfilled.

The perfectly disciplined man is always in tune with the wish as an accomplished fact. He knows that consciousness is the one and only reality, that ideas and feelings are facts of consciousness and are as real as objects in space; therefore he never entertains a feeling which does not contribute to his happiness, for feelings are the causes of the actions and circumstances of his life.

The Wish Fulfilled

All that is necessary is to create a passive state and feel the wish fulfilled.

All you can possibly need or desire is already yours. You need no helper to give it to you; it is yours now. Call your desires into being by imagining and feeling your wish fulfilled.

As the end is accepted, you become totally indifferent as to possible failure, for acceptance of the end wills the means to that end. When you emerge from the moment of prayer, it is as though you were shown the happy and successful end of a play although you were not shown how that end was achieved.

However, having witnessed the end, regardless of any anticlimactic sequence, you remain calm and secure in the knowledge that the end has been perfectly defined.

The Wish Fulfilled

"Be ye transformed by the renewing of your mind."

To be transformed, the whole basis of your thoughts must change. But your thoughts cannot change unless you have new ideas, for you think from your ideas.

All transformation begins with an intense, burning desire to be transformed. The first step in the

"renewing of the mind"

is desire. You must want to be different, and intend to be, before you can begin to change yourself. Then you must make your future dream a present fact.

You do this by assuming the feeling of your wish fulfilled. By desiring to be other than what you are, you can create an ideal of the person you want to be and assume that you are already that person. If this assumption is persisted in until it becomes your dominant feeling, the attainment of your ideal is inevitable.

The ideal you hope to achieve is always ready for an incarnation, but unless you yourself offer it human parentage, it is incapable of birth.

Therefore, your attitude should be one in which having desired to express a higher state . . you alone accept the task of incarnating this new and greater value of yourself.

In giving birth to your ideal, you must bear in mind that the methods of mental and spiritual knowledge are entirely different.

This is a point that is truly understood by probably not more than one person in a million.

The Wish Fulfilled

You must be conscious of being secure if you are to know what security is.

Therefore, to incarnate a new and greater value of yourself, you must assume that you already are what you want to be and then live by faith in this assumption, which is not yet incarnate in the body of your life, in confidence that this new value or state of consciousness will become incarnated through your absolute fidelity to the assumption that you are that which you desire to be.

This is what wholeness means, what integrity means.

They mean submission of the whole self to the feeling of the wish fulfilled in certainty that that new state of consciousness is the renewing of mind which transforms. There is no order in Nature corresponding to this willing submission of the self to the ideal beyond the self.

Therefore, it is the height of folly to expect the incarnation of a new and greater concept of self to come about by natural evolutionary process.

That which requires a state of consciousness to produce its effect obviously cannot be effected without such a state of consciousness, and in your ability to assume the feeling of a greater life, to assume a new concept of yourself, you possess what the rest of Nature does not possess . . imagination . . the instrument by which you create your world.

The Wish Fulfilled

The changes which take place in your life as a result of your changed concept of yourself always appear to the unenlightened to be the result, not of a change of your consciousness, but of chance, outer cause, or coincidence.

However, the only fate governing your life is the fate determined by your own concepts, your own assumptions; for an assumption, though false, if persisted in, will harden into fact.

The ideal you seek and hope to attain will not manifest itself, will not be realized by you until you have imagined that you are already that ideal.

There is no escape for you except by a radical psychological transformation of yourself, except by your assumption of the feeling of your wish fulfilled. Therefore, make results or accomplishments the crucial test of your ability to use your imagination.

Everything depends on your attitude towards yourself. That which you will not affirm as true of yourself can never be realized by you, for that attitude alone is the necessary condition by which you realize your goal.

The Wish Fulfilled

All transformation is based upon suggestion, and this can work only where you lay yourself completely open to an influence.

You must abandon yourself to your ideal as a woman abandons herself to love, for complete abandonment of self to it is the way to union with your ideal.

You must assume the feeling of the wish fulfilled until your assumption has all the sensory vividness of reality. You must imagine that you are already experiencing what you desire. That is, you must assume the feeling of the fulfillment of your desire until you are possessed by it and this feeling crowds all other ideas out of your consciousness.

The man who is not prepared for the conscious plunge into the assumption of the wish fulfilled in the faith that it is the only way to the realization of his dream is not yet ready to live consciously by the law of assumption, although there is no doubt that he does live by the law of assumption unconsciously.

But for you, who accept this principle and are ready to live by consciously assuming that your wish is already fulfilled, the adventure of life begins.

To reach a higher level of being, you must assume a higher concept of yourself. If you will not imagine yourself as other than what you are, then you remain as you are,

"for if ye believe not that I AM He,
ye shall die in your sins."

If you do not believe that you are He, the person you want to be, then you remain as you are.

Through the faithful systematic cultivation of the feeling of the wish fulfilled, desire becomes the promise of its own fulfillment.

The assumption of the feeling of the wish fulfilled makes the future dream a present fact.

The Wish Fulfilled

The great secret is a controlled imagination and a well sustained attention firmly and repeatedly focused on the object to be accomplished. It cannot be emphasized too much that, by creating an ideal within your mental sphere, by assuming that you are already that ideal, you identify yourself with it and thereby transform yourself into its image, thinking from the ideal instead of thinking of the ideal.

Every state is already there as "mere possibilities" as long as we think of them, but as overpoweringly real when we think from them.

This was called by the ancient teachers

"Subjection to the will of God"

or

"Resting in the Lord",

and the only true test of "Resting in the Lord" is that all who do rest are inevitably transformed into the image of that in which they rest, thinking from the wish fulfilled.

You become according to your resigned will, and your resigned will is your concept of yourself and all that you consent to and accept as true. You, assuming the feeling of your wish fulfilled and continuing therein, take upon yourself the results of that state; not assuming the feeling of your wish fulfilled, you are ever free of the results.

When you understand the redemptive function of imagination, you hold in your hands the key to the solution of all your problems.

Every phase of your life is made by the exercise of your imagination. Determined imagination alone is the means of your progress, of the fulfilling of your dreams. It is the beginning and end of all creating.

The Wish Fulfilled

The desire which realizes itself is always a desire upon which attention is exclusively concentrated, for an idea is endowed with power only in proportion to the degree of attention fixed on it.

Concentrated observation is the attentive attitude directed from some specific end. The attentive attitude involves selection, for when you pay attention, it signifies that you have decided to focus your attention on one object or state rather than on another.

Therefore, when you know what you want, you must deliberately focus your attention on the feeling of your wish fulfilled until that feeling fills the mind and crowds all other ideas out of consciousness.

The power of attention is the measure of your inner force.

Concentrated observation of one thing shuts out other things and causes them to disappear. The great secret of success is to focus the attention on the feeling of the wish fulfilled without permitting any distraction.

All progress depends upon an increase of attention.

The Wish Fulfilled

This one thing I do, forgetting those things that are behind, I press toward the mark.

This means you, this one thing you can do,

"forgetting those things that are behind".

You can press toward the mark of filling your mind with the feeling of the wish fulfilled.

To the unenlightened man, this will seem to be all fantasy, yet all progress comes from those who do not take the accepted view, nor accept the world as it is.

As was stated heretofore, if you can imagine what you please, and if the forms of your thought are as vivid as the forms of nature, you are, by virtue of the power of your imagination, master of your fate.

"Your imagination is you yourself, and the world as your imagination sees it, is the real world."

The Wish Fulfilled

Imagination is able to do anything, but only according to the internal direction of your attention.

If you persist night after night, sooner or later you will awaken in yourself a center of power and become conscious of your greater self, the real you.

Attention is developed by repeated exercise or habit. Through habit, an action becomes easier, and so, in course of time, gives rise to a facility or faculty, which can then be put to higher uses.

When you attain control of the internal direction of your attention, you will no longer stand in shallow water, but will launch out into the deep of life.

You will walk in the assumption of the wish fulfilled as on a foundation more solid even than earth.

The Wish Fulfilled

Since what we believe to be the "real" physical world is actually only an "assumptive" world, it is not surprising that these experiments prove that what appears to be solid reality is actually the result of "expectations" or "assumptions".

Your assumptions determine not only what you see, but also what you do, for they govern all your conscious and subconscious movements towards the fulfillment of themselves.

Over a century ago, this truth was stated by Emerson as follows:

> As the world was plastic and fluid in the hands of God, so it is ever to so much of his attributes as we bring to it. To ignorance and sin, it is flint. They adapt themselves to it as they may, but in proportion as a man has anything in him divine, the firmament flows before him and takes his signet and form.

Your assumption is the hand of God molding the firmament into the image of that which you assume. The assumption of the wish fulfilled is the high tide which lifts you easily off the bar of the senses where you have so long lain stranded. It lifts the mind into prophecy in the full right sense of the word; and if you have that controlled imagination and absorbed attention which it is possible to attain, you may be sure that all your assumption implies will come to pass.

The Wish Fulfilled

An assumption builds a bridge of incidents that lead inevitably to the fulfillment of itself.

Man believes the future to be the natural development of the past. But the law of assumption clearly shows that this is not the case. Your assumption places you psychologically where you are not physically; then your senses pull you back from where you were psychologically to where you are physically. It is these psychological forward motions that produce your physical forward motions in time. Precognition permeates all the scriptures of the world.

*"In my Father's house are many mansions;
If it were not so, I would have told you. I
go to prepare a place for you. And if I go
and prepare a place for you, I will come
again and receive you unto myself:
that where I am, there ye may be also...
And now I have told you before it came
to pass, that, when it is come to pass,
ye might believe."*

The "I" in this quotation is your imagination, which goes into the future, into one of the many mansions. Mansion is the state desired... telling of an event before it occurs physically is simply feeling yourself into the state desired until it has the tone of reality. You go and prepare a place for yourself by imagining yourself into the feeling of your wish fulfilled.

Then, you speed from this state of the wish fulfilled, where you have not been physically, back to where you were physically a moment ago. Then, with an irresistible forward movement, you move forward across a series of events to the physical realization of your wish, that where you have been in imagination, there you will be in the flesh also.

*"Unto the place from whence the rivers
come, thither they return again.*

The Wish Fulfilled

The whole of creation exists in you, and it is your destiny to become increasingly aware of its infinite wonders and to experience ever greater and grander portions of it.

If creation is finished, and all events are taking place now, the question that springs naturally to the mind is

"what determines your time track?"

That is, what determines the events which you encounter?

And the answer is your concept of yourself. Concepts determine the route that attention follows.

Here is a good test to prove this fact. Assume the feeling of your wish fulfilled and observe the route that your attention follows. You will observe that as long as you remain faithful to your assumption, so long will your attention be confronted with images clearly related to that assumption.

The Wish Fulfilled

Whenever you become completely absorbed in an emotional state, you are at that moment assuming the feeling of the state fulfilled.

If persisted in, whatsoever you are intensely emotional about, you will experience in your world. These periods of absorption, of concentrated attention, are the beginnings of the things you harvest.

It is in such moments that you are exercising your creative power, the only creative power there is.

At the end of these periods, or moments of absorption, you speed from these imaginative states (where you have not been physically) to where you were physically an instant ago.

In these periods, the imagined state is so real that, when you return to the objective world and find that it is not the same as the imagined state, it is an actual shock.

You have seen something in imagination with such vividness that you now wonder whether the evidence of your senses can now be believed,

and, like Keats, you ask,

"was it a vision
or a waking dream?
Fled is that music...
Do I wake or sleep?"

This shock reverses your time sense. By this is meant that instead of your experience resulting from your past, it now becomes the result of being in imagination where you have not yet been physically.

In effect, this moves you across a bridge of incident to the physical realization of your imagined state.

The man who at will can assume whatever state he pleases has found the keys to the Kingdom of Heaven.

The keys are desire, imagination, and a steadily focused attention on the feeling of the wish fulfilled.

To such a man, any undesirable objective fact is no longer a reality and the ardent wish no longer a dream.

The Wish Fulfilled

"Prove Me now herewith, saith the Lord of hosts, if I will not open you the windows of heaven, and pour you out a blessing, that there shall not be room enough to receive it."

The windows of heaven may not be opened and the treasures seized by a strong will, but they open of themselves and present their treasures as a free gift, a gift that comes when absorption reaches such a degree that it results in a feeling of complete acceptance.

The passage from your present state to the feeling of your wish fulfilled is not across a gap. There is continuity between the so-called real and unreal.

To cross from one state to the other, you simply extend your feelers, trust your touch and enter fully into the spirit of what you are doing.

"Not by might nor by power, but by My Spirit, saith the Lord of hosts."

Assume the spirit, the feeling of the wish fulfilled, and you will have opened the windows to receive the blessing.

To assume a state is to get into the spirit of it. Your triumphs will be a surprise only to those who did not know your hidden passage from the state of longing to the assumption of the wish fulfilled.

The Lord of hosts will not respond to your wish until you have assumed the feeling of already being what you want to be, for acceptance is the channel of His action.

Acceptance is the Lord of hosts in action.

The Wish Fulfilled

The day you fully realize the power of assumption, you discover that it works in complete conformity with this principle. It works by means of attention, minus effort. Thus, with least action, through an assumption, you hurry without haste and reach your goal without effort.

Because creation is finished, what you desire already exists.

It is excluded from view because you can see only the contents of your own consciousness. It is the function of an assumption to call back the excluded view and restore full vision.

It is not the world, but your assumptions that change. An assumption brings the invisible into sight. It is nothing more nor less than seeing with the eye of God, i.e., imagination.

"For the Lord seeth not as a man seeth,
for man looketh on the outward appearance,
but the Lord looketh on the heart."

The heart is the primary organ of sense, hence the first cause of experience. When you look "on the heart", you are looking at your assumptions: assumptions determine your experience. Watch your assumption with all diligence, for out of it are the issues of life. Assumptions have the power of objective realization.

Every event in the visible world is the result of an assumption or idea in the unseen world.

The present moment is all-important, for it is only in the present moment that our assumptions can be controlled.

The future must become the present in your mind if you would wisely operate the law of assumption. The future becomes the present when you imagine that you already are what you will be when your assumption is fulfilled.

Be still (least action) and know that you are that which you desire to be.

The end of longing should be Being. Translate your dream into Being. Perpetual construction of future states without the consciousness of already being them, that is, picturing your desire without actually assuming the feeling of the wish fulfilled, is the fallacy and mirage of mankind.

It is simply futile day-dreaming.

The Wish Fulfilled

The great secret is a controlled imagination and a well sustained attention firmly and repeatedly focused on the feeling of the wish fulfilled until it fills the mind and crowds all other ideas out of consciousness.

What greater gifts could be given you than to be told the Truth that will set you free?

The Truth that sets you free is that you can experience in imagination what you desire to experience in reality, and by maintaining this experience in imagination, your desire will become an actuality.

You are limited only by your uncontrolled imagination and lack of attention to the feeling of your wish fulfilled. When the imagination is not controlled and the attention not steadied on the feeling of the wish fulfilled, then no amount of prayer or piety or invocation will produce the desired effect.

When you can call up at will whatsoever image you please, when the forms of your imagination are as vivid to you as the forms of nature, you are master of your fate.

The Wish Fulfilled

The assumption of the wish fulfilled is the ship that carries you over the unknown seas to the fulfillment of your dream.

The assumption is everything; realization is subconscious and effortless.

"Assume a virtue if you have it not."

Act on the assumption that you already possess that which you sought.

"Blessed is she that believed; for there shall be a performance of those things which were told her from the Lord."

As the Immaculate Conception is the foundation of the Christian mysteries, so the Assumption is their crown.

Psychologically, the Immaculate Conception means the birth of an idea in your own consciousness, unaided by another.

The Wish Fulfilled

Every man is the Mary of the Immaculate Conception and birth to his idea must give. The Assumption is the crown of the mysteries because it is the highest use of consciousness. When in imagination you assume the feeling of the wish fulfilled, you are mentally lifted up to a higher level.

When, through your persistence, this assumption becomes actual fact, you automatically find yourself on a higher level, that is, you have achieved your desire, in your objective world.

Your assumption guides all your conscious and subconscious movements towards its suggested end so inevitably that it actually dictates the events.

The drama of life is a psychological one and the whole of it is written and produced by your assumptions.

Learn the art of assumption, for only in this way can you create your own happiness.

The Wish Fulfilled

Since creation is finished, it is impossible to force anything into being.

The example of magnetism previously given is a good illustration. You cannot make magnetism; it can only be displayed. You cannot make the law of magnetism.

If you want to build a magnet, you can do so only by conforming to the law of magnetism. In other words, you surrender yourself, or yield to the law. In like manner, when you use the faculty of assumption, you are conforming to a law just as real as the law governing magnetism.

You can neither create nor change the law of assumption.

It is in this respect that you are impotent. You can only yield or conform, and since all of your experiences are the result of your assumptions, consciously or unconsciously, the value of consciously using the power of assumption surely must be obvious.

Willingly identify yourself with that which you most desire, knowing that it will find expression through you.

Yield to the feeling of the wish fulfilled and be consumed as its victim, then rise as the prophet of the law of assumption.

The Wish Fulfilled

It is of great significance that the truth of the principles outlined in this book have been proven time and again by the personal experiences of the Author.

Throughout the past twenty-five years, he has applied these principles and proved them successful in innumerable instances. He attributes to an unwavering assumption of his wish already being fulfilled every success that he has achieved.

He was confident that, by these fixed assumptions, his desires were predestined to be fulfilled. Time and again, he assumed the feeling of his wish fulfilled and continued in his assumption until that which he desired was completely realized.

Live your life in a sublime spirit of confidence and determination; disregard appearances, conditions, in fact all evidence of your senses that deny the fulfillment of your desire.

Rest in the assumption that you are already what you want to be, for, in that determined assumption, you and your Infinite Being are merged in creative unity, and with your Infinite Being (God) all things are possible. God never fails.

"For who can stay His hand or say unto Him, What doest thou?"

Through the mastery of your assumptions, you are in very truth enabled to master life.

The Wish Fulfilled

"He calleth things that are not seen as though they were, and the unseen becomes seen".

Each assumption has its corresponding world.

If you are truly observant, you will notice the power of your assumptions to change circumstances which appear wholly immutable.

You, by your conscious assumptions, determine the nature of the world in which you live.

Ignore the present state and assume the wish fulfilled.

Claim it; it will respond.

The law of assumption is the means by which the fulfillment of your desires may be realized.

Every moment of your life, consciously or unconsciously, you are assuming a feeling. You can no more avoid assuming a feeling than you can avoid eating and drinking.

All you can do is control the nature of your assumptions. Thus it is clearly seen that the control of your assumption is the key you now hold to an ever expanding, happier, more noble life.

The Wish Fulfilled

"Be ye doers of the word and not hearers only, deceiving your own selves. For if any be a hearer of the word, and not a doer, he is like unto a man beholding his natural face in a glass and goeth his way, and straightway forgetteth what manner of man he was. But whoso looketh into the perfect law of liberty, and continue therein, he being not a forgetful hearer but a doer of the work, this man shall be blessed in his deed."

The word, in this quotation, means idea, concept, or desire.

You deceive yourself by "hearing only" when you expect your desire to be fulfilled through mere wishful thinking.

Your desire is what you want to be, and looking at yourself "in a glass" is seeing yourself in imagination as that person.

Forgetting "what manner of man" you are is failing to persist in your assumption.

The "perfect law of liberty" is the law which makes possible liberation from limitation, that is, the law of assumption. To continue in the perfect law of liberty is to persist in the assumption that your desire is already fulfilled.

You are not a "forgetful hearer" when you keep the feeling of your wish fulfilled constantly alive in your consciousness.

This makes you a "doer of the work", and you are blessed in your deed by the inevitable realization of your desire.

You must be doers of the law of assumption, for without application, the most profound understanding will not produce any desired result. Frequent reiteration and repetition of important basic truths runs through these pages.

Where the law of assumption is concerned . . the law that sets man free . . this is a good thing. It should be made clear again and again even at the risk of repetition. The real truth-seeker will welcome this aid in concentrating his attention upon the law which sets him free.

The Wish Fulfilled

Experience in your imagination what you would experience in reality had you achieved your goal.

You must gain it in imagination first, for imagination is the very door to the reality of that which you seek. But use imagination masterfully and not as an onlooker thinking of the end, but as a partaker thinking from the end.

Imagine that you possess a quality or something you desire which hitherto has not been yours. Surrender yourself completely to this feeling until your whole being is possessed by it.

This state differs from reverie in this respect:

it is the result of a controlled imagination and a steadied, concentrated attention, whereas reverie is the result of an uncontrolled imagination . . usually just a daydream.

In the controlled state, a minimum of effort suffices to keep your consciousness filled with the feeling of the wish fulfilled. The physical and mental immobility of this state is a powerful aid to voluntary attention and a major factor of minimum effort.

The Wish Fulfilled

The question is often asked,

"What should be done between the assumption of the wish fulfilled and its realization?"

Nothing.

It is a delusion that, other than assuming the feeling of the wish fulfilled, you can do anything to aid the realization of your desire.

You think that you can do something, you want to do something; but actually you can do nothing.

The illusion of the free will to do, is but ignorance of the law of assumption, upon which all action is based.

Everything happens automatically.

All that befalls you, all that is done by you . . happens.

Your assumptions, conscious or unconscious, direct all thought and action to their fulfillment.

To understand the law of assumption, to be convinced of its truth, means getting rid of all the illusions about free will to act.

Free will actually means freedom to select any idea you desire.

By assuming the idea already to be a fact, it is converted into reality. Beyond that, free will ends, and everything happens in harmony with the concept assumed.

The Wish Fulfilled

You are a being with powers of intervention, which enable you, by a change of consciousness, to alter the course of observed events, in fact, to change your future.

Deny the evidence of the senses, and assume the feeling of the wish fulfilled.

Inasmuch as your assumption is creative and forms an atmosphere, your assumption, if it be a noble one, increases your assurance and helps you to reach a higher level of being.

If, on the other hand, your assumption be an unlovely one, it hinders you and makes your downward way swifter. Just as the lovely assumptions create a harmonious atmosphere, so the hard and bitter feelings create a hard and bitter atmosphere.

"Whatsoever things are pure, just, lovely, of good report, think on these things."

This means to make your assumptions the highest, noblest, happiest concepts. There is no better time to start than now. The present moment is always the most opportune in which to eliminate all unlovely assumptions and to concentrate only on the good.

The Wish Fulfilled

You must assume that you are what you want to be and continue therein, for the reality of your assumption has its being, in complete independence of objective fact and will clothe itself in flesh if you persist in the feeling of the wish fulfilled.

When you know that assumptions, if persisted in, harden into facts, then events which seem to the uninitiated mere accidents will be understood by you to be the logical and inevitable effects of your assumption.

The important thing to bear in mind is that you have infinite free will in choosing your assumptions, but no power to determine conditions and events.

You can create nothing, but your assumption determines what portion of creation you will experience.

The Wish Fulfilled

"Man ought always to pray and not to faint."

Here, to pray means to give thanks for already having what you desire.

Only persistency in the assumption of the wish fulfilled can cause those subtle changes in your mind which result in the desired change in your life. It matters not whether they be "Angels", "Elisha", or "reluctant judges"; all must respond in harmony with your persistent assumption.

When it appears that people other than yourself in your world do not act toward you as you would like, it is not due to reluctance on their part, but a lack of persistence in your assumption of your life already being as you want it to be.

Your assumption, to be effective, cannot be a single isolated act; it must be a maintained attitude of the wish fulfilled.

And that maintained attitude that gets you there, so that you think from your wish fulfilled instead of thinking about your wish, is aided by assuming the feeling of the wish fulfilled frequently.

It is the frequency, not the length of time, that makes it natural. That to which you constantly return constitutes your truest self.

Frequent occupancy of the feeling of the wish fulfilled is the secret of success.

The Wish Fulfilled

Suppose that I desire to be in some other place or situation. Could I, by imagining myself into such a state and place, bring about their physical realization?

Suppose I could not afford the journey and suppose my present social and financial status oppose the idea that I want to realize. Would imagination be sufficient of itself to incarnate these desires? Does imagination comprehend reason? By reason, I mean deductions from the observations of the senses.

Does it recognize the external world of facts?

In the practical way of everyday life is imagination a complete guide to behavior?

Suppose I am capable of acting with continuous imagination, that is, suppose I am capable of sustaining the feeling of my wish fulfilled, will my assumption harden into fact?

And, if it does harden into fact, shall I on reflection find that my actions through the period of incubation have been reasonable? Is my imagination a power sufficient, not merely to assume the feeling of the wish fulfilled, but is it also of itself capable of incarnating the idea?

After assuming that I am already what I want to be, must I continually guide myself by reasonable ideas and actions in order to bring about the fulfillment of my assumption?

Experience has convinced me that an assumption, though false, if persisted in, will harden into fact, that continuous imagination is sufficient for all things, and all my reasonable plans and actions will never make up for my lack of continuous imagination.

The Wish Fulfilled

It was in the fall of 1933 in New York City that I approached Abdullah with a problem. He asked me one simple question,

"What do you want?"

I told him that I would like to spend the winter in Barbados, but that I was broke. I literally did not have a nickel.

"If you will imagine yourself to be in Barbados", said he, "thinking and viewing the world from that state of consciousness instead of thinking of Barbados, you will spend the winter there."

"You must not concern yourself with the ways and means of getting there, for the state of consciousness of already being in Barbados, if occupied by your imagination, will devise the means best suited to realize itself."

Man lives by committing himself to invisible states, by fusing his imagination with what he knows to be other than himself, and in this union he experiences the results of that fusion. No one can lose what he has, save by detachment from the state where the things experienced have their natural life.

"You must imagine yourself right into the state of your fulfilled desire", Abdullah told me, "and fall asleep viewing the world from Barbados."

The world which we describe from observation must be as we describe it relative to ourselves.

Our imagination connects us with the state desired. But we must use imagination masterfully, not as an onlooker thinking of the end, but as a partaker thinking from the end. We must actually be there in imagination.

If we do this, our subjective experience will be realized objectively.

"This is not mere fancy", said he, "but a truth you can prove by experience."

His appeal to enter into the wish fulfilled was the secret of thinking from the end. Every state is already there as "mere possibility" as long as you think of it, but is overpoweringly real when you think from it.

The Wish Fulfilled

I, by the intensity of my imagination and feeling, imagining and feeling myself to be in Barbados instead of merely thinking of Barbados, had spanned the vast

Atlantic to influence my brother into desiring my presence to complete the family circle at Christmas.

Thinking from the end, from the feeling of my wish fulfilled, was the source of everything that happened as outer cause, such as my brother's impulse to send me a steamship ticket; and it was also the cause of everything that appeared as results.

In Ideas of Good and Evil, W. B. Yeats, having described a few experiences similar to this experience of mine, writes:

> If all who have described events like this have not dreamed, we should rewrite our histories, for all men, certainly all imaginative men, must be forever casting forth enchantments, glamour, illusions; and all men, especially tranquil men who have no powerful egotistic life, must be continually passing under their power.

Determined imagination, thinking from the end, is the beginning of all miracles.

I would like to give you an immense belief in miracles, but a miracle is only the name given by those who have no knowledge of the power and function of imagination to the works of imagination.

Imagining oneself into the feeling of the wish fulfilled is the means by which a new state is entered. This gives the state the quality of is-ness.

The Wish Fulfilled

There is no stopping the man who can think from the end. Nothing can stop him. He creates the means and grows his way out of limitation into ever greater and greater mansions of the Lord. It does not matter what he has been or what he is.

All that matters is

"what does he want?"

He knows that the world is a manifestation of the mental activity which goes on within himself, so he strives to determine and control the ends from which he thinks.

In his imagination he dwells in the end, confident that he shall dwell there in the flesh also. He puts his whole trust in the feeling of the wish fulfilled and lives by committing himself to that state, for the art of fortune is to tempt him so to do.

Like the man at the pool of Bethesda, he is ready for the moving of the waters of imagination. Knowing that every desire is ripe grain to him who knows how to think from the end, he is indifferent to mere reasonable probability and confident that through continuous imagination his assumptions will harden into fact.

But how to persuade men everywhere that thinking from the end is the only living, how to foster it in every activity of man, how to reveal it as the plenitude of life and not the compensation of the disappointed: that is the problem.

Life is a controllable thing.

The Wish Fulfilled

Man attracts what he is. The art of life is to sustain the feeling of the wish fulfilled and let things come to you, not to go after them or think they flee away.

Observe your inner talking and remember your aim. Do they match? Does your inner talking match what you would say audibly had you achieved your goal?

The individual's inner speech and actions attract the conditions of his life. Through uncritical self-observation of your inner talking you find where you are in the inner world, and where you are in the inner world is what you are in the outer world. You put on the new man whenever ideals and inner speech match. In this way alone can the new man be born.

Inner talking matures in the dark. From the dark it issues into the light. The right inner speech is the speech that would be yours were you to realize your ideal.

In other words, it is the speech of fulfilled desire.

"I AM that."

The Wish Fulfilled

When reason and the facts of life oppose the idea you desire to realize and you accept the evidence of your senses and the dictates of reason as the truth, you have brought the Lord, your consciousness, the gift of Cain.

It is obvious that such offerings do not please Him.

Life on earth is a training ground for image making. If you use only the molds which your senses dictate, there will be no change in your life.

You are here to live the more abundant life, so you must use the invisible molds of imagination and make results and accomplishments the crucial test of your power to create. Only as you assume the feeling of the wish fulfilled and continue therein are you offering the gift that pleases.

"When Abel's gift is my attire
Then I'll realize my desire."
The Prophet Malachi complains
that man has robbed God:
"But ye say, Wherein have we
robbed thee? In tithes and offerings."

Facts based upon reason and the evidence of the senses which oppose the idea seeking expression, rob you of the belief in the reality of the invisible state. But

"faith is the evidence of things not seen",

and through it

Good calleth those things which be not as though they were . . .

Call the thing not seen; assume the feeling of your wish fulfilled.

The Wish Fulfilled

"And, I, if I be lifted up from the earth,
will draw all men unto me."

If I be lifted up from the evidence of the senses to the state of consciousness I desire to realize and remain in that state until it feels natural, I will form that state around me and all men will see it.

But how to persuade man this is true . . that imaginative life is the only living; that assuming the feeling of the wish fulfilled is the way to the more abundant life and not the compensation of the escapist, that is the problem.

To see as

"though widening chambers of delight"

what living in the realms of imagination means, to appreciate and enjoy the world, one must live imaginatively; one must dream and occupy his dream, then grow and outgrow the dream, forever and ever.

The unimaginative man, who will not lose his life on one level that he may find it on a higher level, is nothing but a Lot's wife, a pillar of self-satisfied salt.

On the other hand, those who refuse form as being unspiritual and who reject incarnation as separate from God are ignorant of the great mystery:

"Great is the mystery, God was manifest in the flesh."

Your life expresses one thing, and one thing only, your state of consciousness.

Everything is dependent upon that. As you, through the medium of imagination, assume a state of consciousness, that state begins to clothe itself in form, It solidifies around you as the serpent's skin ossifies around it. But you must be faithful to the state. You must not go from state to state, but, rather, wait patiently in the one invisible state until it takes on form and becomes an objective fact.

Patience is necessary, but patience will be easy after your first success in shedding the old and growing the new, for we are able to wait according as we have been rewarded by understanding in the past.

Understanding is the secret of patience.

The Wish Fulfilled

Whatever you desire is already

"furnished and prepared".

Your imagination can put you in touch inwardly with that state of consciousness. If you imagine that you are already the one you want to be,

you are following the

"man bearing a pitcher of water".

If you remain in that state, you have entered the guest-chamber . . Passover . . and committed your spirit into the hands of God . . your consciousness.

A man's state of consciousness is his demand on the Infinite Store House of God, and, like the law of commerce, a demand creates a supply.

To change the supply, you change the demand . . your state of consciousness.

What you desire to be, that you must feel you already are. Your state of consciousness creates the conditions of your life, rather than the conditions create your state of consciousness.

To know this Truth, is to have the

"water of life".

But your savior . . the solution of your problem . . cannot be manifested by such knowledge only.

It can be realized only as such knowledge is applied.

Only as you assume the feeling of your wish fulfilled, and continue therein, is your side pierced;

"from whence cometh blood and water".

In this manner only is Jesus, the solution of your problem, realized.

The Wish Fulfilled

God is your consciousness.

His promises are conditional. Unless the demand, your state of consciousness, is changed, the supply . . the present conditions of your life, remain as they are.

"As we forgive"

as we change our mind, the law is automatic. Your state of consciousness is the spring of action, the directing force, and that which creates the supply.

"If that nation, against whom
I have pronounced, turn from
their evil, I will repent of the
evil that I thought to do unto them.
And at what instant I shall speak
concerning a nation, and concerning
a kingdom, to build and to
plant it;

If it do evil in my sight, that it
obey not my voice, then I will
repent of the good, wherewith I
said I would benefit them."

This statement of Jeremiah suggests that a commitment is involved if the individual or nation would realize the goal, a commitment to certain fixed attitudes of mind.

The feeling of the wish fulfilled is a necessary condition in mans search for the goal.

The Wish Fulfilled

Imagining creates events.

The world, created out of men's imagining, comprises un-numbered warring beliefs; therefore, there can never be a perfectly stable or static state. Today's events are bound to disturb yesterday's established order. Imaginative men and women invariably unsettle a preexisting peace of mind.

Do not bow before the dictate of facts and accept life on the basis of the world without. Assert the supremacy of your Imaginal acts over facts and put all things in subjection to them.

Hold fast to your ideal in your imagination. Nothing can take it from you but your failure to persist in imagining the ideal realized.

Imagine only such states that are of value or promise well.

To attempt to change circumstances before you change your imaginal activity, is to struggle against the very nature of things. There can be no outer change until there is first an imaginal change.

Everything you do, unaccompanied by an imaginal change, is but futile readjustment of surfaces. Imagining the wish fulfilled brings about a union with that state, and during that union you behave in keeping with your imaginal change.

This shows you that an imaginal change will result in a change of behavior. However, your ordinary imaginal alterations as you pass from one state to another are not transformations because each of them is so rapidly succeeded by another in the reverse direction.

But whenever one state grows so stable as to become your constant mood, your habitual attitude, then that habitual state defines your character and is a true transformation.

The Wish Fulfilled

You must abandon yourself mentally to your wish fulfilled in your love for that state, and in so doing, live in the new state and no more in the old state.

You can't commit yourself to what you do not love, so the secret of self-commission is faith, plus love. Faith is believing what is unbelievable. Commit yourself to the feeling of the wish fulfilled, in faith, that this act of self-commission, will become a reality. And it must become a reality because imagining creates reality.

Imagination is both conservative and transformative. It is conservative when it builds its world from images supplied by memory and the evidence of the senses.

It is creatively transformative when it imagines things as they ought to be, building its world out of the generous dreams of fancy.

In the procession of images, the ones that take precedence, naturally, are those of the senses. Nevertheless, a present sense impression is only an image. It does not differ in nature from a memory image or the image of a wish. What makes a present sense impression so objectively real is the individual's imagination functioning in it and thinking from it; whereas, in a memory image or a wish, the individual's imagination is not functioning in it and thinking from it, but is functioning out of it and thinking of it.

If you would enter into the image in your imagination, then would you know what it is to be creatively transformative: then would you realize your wish; and then you would be happy.

Every image can be embodied. But unless you, yourself, enter the image and think from it, it is incapable of birth. Therefore, it is the height of folly to expect the wish to be realized by the mere passage of time.

That which requires imaginative occupancy to produce its effect, obviously cannot be effected without such occupancy. You cannot be in one image and not suffer the consequences of not being in another.

Imagination is spiritual sensation. Enter the image of the wish fulfilled, then give it sensory vividness and tones of reality by mentally acting as you would act were it a physical fact.

The Wish Fulfilled

"My God, I heard this day,
that none doth build a stately habitation,
but he that means to dwell therein.
What house more stately hath there been,
or can be, than is Man?
to whose creation all things are in decay."
. . . George Herbert

I wish it were true of man's noble dreams, but unfortunately, perpetual construction, deferred occupancy, is the common fault of man.

Why

"build a stately habitation,"

unless you intend to

"dwell therein?"

Why build a dream house and not

"dwell therein?"

This is the secret of those who lie in bed awake while they dream things true. They know how to live in their dream until, in fact, they do just that.

Man, through the medium of a controlled, waking dream, can predetermine his future. That imaginal activity, of living in the feeling of the wish fulfilled, leads man across a bridge of incident to the fulfillment of the dream.

If we live in the dream, thinking from it, and not of it, then the creative power of imagining will answer our adventurous fancy, and the wish fulfilled will break in upon us and take us unawares.

Man is all imagination; therefore, man must be where he is in imagination, for his imagination is himself.

The Wish Fulfilled

"... dreamers often lie in bed awake,
while they do dream things true."

One must adopt either the way of imagination or the way of sense. No compromise or neutrality is possible.

"He who is not for me is against me."

When man finally identifies himself with his Imagination rather than his senses, he has at long last discovered the core of reality.

I have often been warned by self-styled "realists" that man will never realize his dream by simply imagining that it is already here.

Yet, man can realize his dream by simply imagining that it is already here.

That is exactly what this collection of stories proves (From "The Law And The Promise"); if only men were prepared to live imaginatively in the feeling of the wish fulfilled, advancing confidently in their controlled waking-dream, then the power of imagining would answer their adventurous fancy and the wish fulfilled would break in upon them and take them unawares.

Nothing is more continuously wonderful than the things that happen every day to the man with imagination sufficiently awake to realize their wonder.

Observe your imaginal activities. Imagine better than the best you know, and create a better world for yourself and others. Live as though the wish had come, even though it is yet to come, and you will shorten the period of waiting.

The world is imaginal, not mechanistic.

Imaginal acts, not blind fate,
determine the course of history.

The Wish Fulfilled

By mentally falsifying the facts of life, man moves from passive reaction to active creation; this breaks the wheel of recurrence and builds a cumulatively enlarging future.

If man does not always create in the full sense of the word, it is because he is not faithful to his vision, or else he thinks of what he wants rather than from his wish fulfilled.

Man is such an extraordinary synthesis, partly tied by his senses, and partly free to dream that his internal conflicts are perennial. The state of conflict in the individual is expressed in society.

Life is a romantic adventure. To live creatively, imagining novel solutions to ever more complex problems is far nobler than to restrain or kill out desire.

All that is desired can be imagined into existence.

"Wouldst thou be in a Dream, and yet not sleep?"

Try to revise your day every night before falling asleep. Try to visualize clearly and enter into the revised scene which would be the imaginal solution of your problem.

The revised imaginal structure may have a great influence on others, but that is not your concern.

The Wish Fulfilled

It is to the pruning shears of revision that we owe our prime fruit. Man and his past are one continuous structure. This structure contains all of the past which has been conserved and still operates below the threshold of his senses to influence the present and the future of his life.

The whole is carrying all of its contents with it; any alteration of content will result in an alteration in the present and the future.

The first act of correction or cure is always "Revise."

If the past can be recreated into the present, so can the revised past. And thus the Revised Past appears within the very heart of her present life; not Fate but a revised past brought her good fortune.

Make results and accomplishment the crucial test of true imagination and your confidence in the power of imagination to create reality will grow gradually from your experiments with revision confronted by experience.

Only by this process of experiment can you realize the potential power of your awakened and controlled imagination.

"How much do you owe my master?"

He said,

"A hundred measures of oil."

And he said to him,

"Take your bill, and sit down quickly and write fifty!"

This parable of the unjust steward urges us to mentally falsify the facts of life, to alter a theme already in being. By means of such imaginative falsehoods, a man "acquires friends."

As each day falls, mentally revise the facts of life and make them conform to events well worthy of recall; tomorrow will take up the altered pattern and go forward until at length it is realized on the heights of attainment.

The reader will find it worthwhile to follow these clues, imaginal construction of scenes implying the wish fulfilled, and imaginative participation in these scenes until tones of reality are reached.

We are dealing with the secret of imagining, in which man is seen awakening into a world completely subject to his imaginative power.

The Wish Fulfilled

"The Nature of Visionary Fancy, or Imagination, is very little known, & the External nature & permanence of its ever Existent Images is consider'd as less permanent than the things of Vegetative & Generative Nature; yet the Oak dies as well as the Lettuce, but Its Eternal image & Individuality never dies, but renews by its seed; just so the Imaginative Image returns by the seed of Contemplative Thought."
. . . Blake

The images of our imagination are the realities of which any physical manifestation is only the shadow.

If we are faithful to vision, the image will create for itself the only physical manifestation of itself it has a right to make.

We speak of the "reality" of a thing when we mean its material substance. That is exactly what an imaginist means by its "unreality" or shadow.

Imagining is spiritual sensation.

Enter into the feeling of your wish fulfilled.

Through spiritual sensation, through your use of imaginal sight, sound, scent, taste and touch, you will give to your image the sensory vividness necessary to produce that image in your outer or shadow world.

The Wish Fulfilled

"This is an age in which the mood decides the fortunes of people rather than the fortunes decide the mood."
. . . Sir Winston Churchill

Men regard their moods far too much as effects and not sufficiently as causes. Moods are imaginal activities without which no creation is possible.

We say that we are happy because we have achieved our goal; we do not realize that the process works equally well in the reverse direction, that we shall achieve our goal because we have assumed the happy feeling of the wish fulfilled.

Moods are not only the result of the conditions of our life; they are also the causes of those conditions.

In "The Psychology of Emotions," Professor Ribot writes,

"An idea which is only an idea produces nothing and does nothing; it only acts if it is felt, if it is accompanied by an effective state, if it awakens tendencies, that is to say, motor elements."

The Wish Fulfilled

The drama of life is an imaginal activity in which we bring to pass by our moods rather than by our physical acts. Moods so ably guide all towards that which they affirm, they may be said to create the circumstances of life and dictate the events.

The mood of the wish fulfilled is the high tide which lifts us easily off the bar of the senses where we usually lie stranded. If we are aware of the mood and know this secret of imagining, we may announce that all that our mood affirms will come to pass.

The Wish Fulfilled

"A man that looks on glass, On it may stay his eye;
Or if he pleaseth, through it pass,
And then the heav'n espy."
. . . George Herbert

Objects, to be perceived, must first penetrate in some manner our brain; but we are not, because of this, interlocked with our environment.

Although normal consciousness is focused on the senses and is usually restricted to them, it is possible for man to pass through his sense fixation into any imaginal structure which he conceives and so fully occupy it, that it is more alive and more responsive than that on which his senses "stay his eye."

If this were not true, man would be an automaton reflecting life, never affecting it.

Man, who is all Imagination, is not tenant to the brain but landlord; he need not rest content with the appearance of things; he can go beyond perceptual to conceptual awareness.

This ability, to pass through the mechanical reflective structure of the senses, is the most important discovery man can make.

It reveals man as a center of imagining with powers of intervention which enable him to alter the course of observed events moving from success to success through a series of mental transformations in himself.

Attention, the spearhead of imagining, may be either attracted from without as his senses "stay his eye" or directed from within "if he pleases" and through the senses pass into the wish fulfilled.

The Wish Fulfilled

"If the Spectator would Enter into these Images in his Imagination, approaching them on the Fiery Chariot of his Contemplative Thought, if he could . . make a Friend & Companion of one of these Images of wonder, which always entreats him to leave mortal things (as he must know) then would he arise from his Grave, then would he meet the Lord in the Air & then he would be happy."

. . . Blake

Imagination, it seems, will do nothing that we wish until we enter into the image of the wish fulfilled.

Does not this entering into the image of the wish fulfilled resemble Blake's "Void outside of Existence which if enter'd into Englobes itself & becomes a Womb?"

Is this not the true interpretation of the mythical story of Adam and Eve? Man and his emanation? Are not man's dreams of fancy his Emanation, his Eve in whom

"He plants himself in all her Nerves,
just as a Husbandman his mold;
And she becomes his dwelling place
and garden fruitful seventy fold?"

The secret of creation is the secret of imagining, first, desiring and then assuming the feeling of the wish fulfilled until the dream of fancy,

'the Void outside existence,'

is enter'd and 'englobes itself and becomes a womb, a dwelling place and garden fruitful seventy fold.'

Note well that Blake urges us to enter info these images. This entering into the image makes it 'englobe itself and become a womb.'

Man, by entering a state impregnates it and causes it to create what the union implies.

Blake tells us that these images are

'Shadowy to those who dwell not in them,
mere possibilities; but to those who enter into them
they seem the only substances. .'

The Wish Fulfilled

"The natural man does not receive the gifts of the Spirit of God, for they are folly to him, and he is not able to understand them because they are spiritually discerned."

"There is a Moment in each Day that Satan cannot find,
Nor can his Watch Fiends find it; but the Industrious
find This Moment & it multiply, & when it once is found
It renovates every Moment of the Day if rightly placed."
. . . Blake

Whenever we imagine things as they ought to be, rather than as they seem to be, is "The Moment."

For in that moment the spiritual man's work is done and all the great events of time start forth to mold a world in harmony with that moment's altered pattern.

Satan, Blake writes, is a "Reactor." He never acts; he only reacts. And if our attitude to the happenings of the day is "reactionary" are we not playing Satan's part?

Man is only reacting in his natural or Satan state; he never acts or creates, he only reacts or recreates. One real creative moment, one real feeling of the wish fulfilled, is worth more than the whole natural life of reaction. In such a moment God's work is done.

Once more we may say with Blake,

"God only Acts and Is, in existing beings or Men."

There is an imaginal past and an imaginal future. If, by reacting, the past is recreated into the present . . so . . by acting out our dreams of fancy, can the future be brought into the present.

"I feel now the future in the instant."

The spiritual man Acts: for him, anything that he wants to do, he can do and do at once, in his imagination, and his motto is always, "The Moment is Now."

"Behold, now is the acceptable time; behold, now is the day of salvation."

Nothing stands between man and the fulfillment of his dream but facts: And facts are the creations of imagining. If man changes his imagining, he will change the facts.

The Wish Fulfilled

The drama of life is a psychological one in which we bring circumstances to pass by our attitudes rather than by our acts.

The cornerstone on which all things are based is mans concept of himself. He acts as he does, and has the experiences that he does, because his concept of himself is what it is, and for no other reason. Had he a different concept of himself, he would act differently and have different experiences.

Man, by assuming the feeling of his wish fulfilled, alters his future in harmony with his assumption, for, assumptions though false, if sustained, will harden into fact.

The undisciplined mind finds it difficult to assume a state which is denied by the senses.

But the ancient teachers discovered that sleep, or a state akin to sleep, aided man in making his assumption.

Therefore, they dramatized the first creative act of man as one in which man was in a profound sleep. This not only sets the pattern for all future creative acts, but shows us that man has but one substance that is truly his to use in creating his world and that is himself.

The Wish Fulfilled

Assume the feeling of the wish fulfilled and go to sleep in this mood.

At night, in a dimensionally larger world, when deep sleep falleth upon men, they see and play the parts that they will later on play on earth.

And the drama is always in harmony with that which their dimensionally greater selves read and play through them. Our illusion of free will is but ignorance of the causes which make us act.

The sensation which dominates the mind of man as he falls asleep, though false, will harden into fact.

Assuming the feeling of the wish fulfilled as we fall asleep, is the command to this embodying process saying to our mood,

"Be thou actual."

In this way we become through a natural process what we desire to be.

The Wish Fulfilled

"In my Father's house are many mansions: if it were not so, I would have told you. I go to prepare a place for you. And if I go and prepare a place for you, I will come again, and receive you unto myself; that where I AM, there ye may be also."

The many mansions are the unnumbered states within your mind, for you are the house of God.

In my Father's house are unnumbered concepts of self.

You could not in eternity exhaust what you are capable of being.

If I sit quietly here and assume that I am elsewhere, I have gone and prepared a place.

But if I open my eyes, the bilocation which I created vanishes and I am back here in the physical form that I left behind me as I went to prepare a place. But I prepared the place nevertheless and will in time dwell there physically.

You do not have to concern yourself with the ways and the means that will be employed to move you across space into that place where you have gone and mentally prepared it. Simply sit quietly, no matter where you are, and mentally actualize it.

But I give you warning, do not treat it lightly, for I am conscious of what it will do to people who treat it lightly. I treated it lightly once because I just wanted to get away, based only upon the temperature of the day.

It was in the deep of winter in New York, and I so desired to be in the warm climate of the Indies, that I slept that night as though I slept under palm trees. Next morning when I awoke it was still very much winter.

I had no intentions of going to the Indies that year, but distressing news came which compelled me to make the journey. It was in the midst of war when ships were being sunk right and left, but I sailed out of New York on a ship 48 hours after I received this news. It was the only way I could get to Barbados, and I arrived just in time to see my mother and say a three-dimensional "Good-bye" to her .

In spite of the fact that I had no intentions of going, the deeper Self watched where the great cloud descended. I placed it in Barbados and this tabernacle (my body) had to go and make the journey to fulfill the command,

"Wherever the sole of your foot shall tread
that have I given unto you."

Wherever the cloud descends in the desert, there you reassemble that tabernacle.

I sailed from New York at midnight on a ship without taking thought of submarines or anything else. I had to go. Things happened in a way that I could not have devised.

I warn you, do not treat it lightly. Do not say, "I will experiment and put myself in Labrador, just to see if it will work." You will go to your Labrador and then you will wonder why you ever came to this class. It will work if you dare assume the feeling of your wish fulfilled as you go to sleep.

The Wish Fulfilled

The only acceptable gift is a joyful heart. Come with singing and praise.

That is the way to come before the Lord, your own consciousness. Assume the feeling of your wish fulfilled, and you have brought the only acceptable gift.

All states of mind other than that of the wish fulfilled are an abomination; they are superstition and mean nothing.

When you come before me, rejoice, because rejoicing implies that something has happened which you desired. Come before me singing, giving praise, and giving thanks, for these states of mind imply acceptance of the state sought.

Put yourself in the proper mood and your own consciousness will embody it.

If I could define prayer for anyone and put it just as clearly as I could, I would simply say,

"It is the feeling of the wish fulfilled."

If you ask, "What do you mean by that?" I would say, "I would feel myself into the situation of the answered prayer and then I would live and act upon that conviction."

I would try to sustain it without effort, that is, I would live and act as though it were already a fact, knowing that as I walk in this fixed attitude my assumption will harden into fact.

The Wish Fulfilled

The key to progress in life and to the fulfillment of dreams lies in ready obedience to its voice. Unhesitating obedience to its voice is an immediate assumption of the wish fulfilled. To desire a state is to have it.

As Pascal has said,

"You would not have sought me had you not already found me."

Man, by assuming the feeling of his wish fulfilled, and then living and acting on this conviction, alters the future in harmony with his assumption. Assumptions awaken what they affirm. As soon as man assumes the feeling of his wish fulfilled, his fourth-dimensional Self finds ways for the attainment of this end, discovers methods for its realization.

I know of no clearer definition of the means by which we realize our desires than to experience in imagination, what we would experience in the flesh, were we to achieve our goal.

This imaginary experience of the end with acceptance, wills the means. The fourth-dimensional Self then constructs with its larger outlook the means necessary to realize the accepted end.

The undisciplined mind finds it difficult to assume a state which is denied by the senses.

But here is a technique that makes it easy to

"call things which are not seen as though they were",

that is, to encounter an event before it occurs. People have a habit of slighting the importance of simple things. But this simple formula for changing the future was discovered after years of searching and experimenting.

The first step in changing the future is desire, that is, define your objective, know definitely what you want.

Second, construct an event which you believe you would encounter following the fulfillment of your desire, an event which implies fulfillment of your desire, something which will have the action of Self predominant.

Third, immobilize the physical body, and induce a condition akin to sleep by imagining that you are sleepy. Lie on a bed, or relax in a chair. Then, with eyelids closed and your attention focused on the action you intend to experience in imagination, mentally feel yourself right into the proposed action; imagining all the while that you are actually performing the action here and now.

You must always participate in the imaginary action; not merely stand back and look on, but feel that you are actually performing the action so that the imaginary sensation is real to you.

It is important always to remember that the proposed action must be one which follows the fulfillment of your desire.

Also you must feel yourself into the action until it has all the vividness and distinctness of reality.

The Wish Fulfilled

The future dream must become a present fact in the mind of him who seeks to realize it.

We must experience in imagination what we would experience in reality in the event we achieved our goal, for the soul imagining itself into a situation takes on the results of that imaginary act.

If it does not imagine itself into a situation, it is ever free of the result.

It is the purpose of this teaching to lift us to a higher state of consciousness, to stir the highest in us to confidence and self-assertion, for that which stirs the highest in us is our teacher and healer.

The very first word of correction or cure is always, "Arise."

If we are to understand the reason for this constant command of the Bible to "arise," we must recognize that the universe understood internally is an infinite series of levels and man is what he is according to where he is in that series.

As we are lifted up in consciousness, our world reshapes itself in harmony with the level to which we are lifted. He who rises from his prayer a better man, his prayer has been granted.

To change the present state we, like Dr. Millikan, must rise to a higher level of consciousness. This rise is accomplished by affirming that we are already that which we want to be;

by assuming the feeling of the wish fulfilled.

The drama of life is a psychological one which we bring to pass by our attitudes rather than by our acts. There is no escape from our present predicament except by a radical psychological transformation. Everything depends upon our attitude towards ourselves.

That which we will not affirm as true of ourselves will not develop in our lives.

The Wish Fulfilled

Always do everything in the present, as though you had it. Always go to the end, as though you had it. The end is where I start from. The minute you say, "Yes, but -" then you don't believe it. You say, you need the money now." Well, I say, "Assume that you have it now." "Ah, but . . "Well, then, you haven't assumed it at all! Walk through the door just as though you had it. You might stumble on it out there. Walk as though you had it. Live in the assumption of the wish fulfilled. Live in it as though it were true.

The Wish Fulfilled

Let me now make it quite clear: You have the gift. You can speak. Even if you were dumb, you still speak . . inwardly you speak, and you form these little speech movements within yourself. Make them conform to your wish fulfilled.

Do what Robert Millikan did when he was a poor boy, and had nothing but a brilliant mind; a great, great understanding of literature; but he had no money, and he was tired of his poverty. And knowing how the mind works, he constructed a sentence that if true would imply he was no longer poor. And his sentence is a beautiful sentence;

"I have," . . not "am going to have"; "I have a lavish, steady, dependable income, consistent with integrity and mutual benefit."

That was the great Robert Millikan, who was the head of Cal-Tech, who gave us his discovery of cosmic rays, who when he died could leave a fortune behind to these charities. I know that the YMCA was one of them; they got a fortune from him. He already settled on his sons and made them financially independent, but he had enough left over to give to his favorite charities, and lived a full, wonderful, marvelous life, where everyone who met him benefited by the actual meeting with that great man. And he started off from "scratch," using this simple technique . . using the simple technique . . using the gift of God that He gave to every person in this world: Mind and Speech.

Whether you be a Frenchman or an American or any other nationality, you have speech and you have a mind. Instead of accepting what you have already done with that gift, you simply ignore it. You brought it into being. All this is solidified speech . . the whole vast manifested world. And you turn from it, and then reconstruct the sentence. Change it, as this one of whom I spoke changed the entire pattern. He was a poor boy, . . the whole family poor, behind the 8-ball financially . . socially and in every sense of the word, behind that 8-ball; and he constructed a scene.

The Wish Fulfilled

So I tell you, you watch carefully what you are saying morning, noon and night. When you go to bed at night, just watch your inner conversations, and see that the sun is not descending upon your anger. Resolve it at that very moment, and make it conform to your wish fulfilled, and make that "wish fulfilled" a. thing of love. What would it be like if it were true? Just what would it be like? Then carry on a conversation from the premise of the wish fulfilled, all clothed in love, for anyone that you think of; and watch how things happen in your world.

The Wish Fulfilled

There is a moment in each day and not just a moment, every moment of time is such a moment if you have a desire. You could actually isolate that moment and then clothe yourself with the feeling of the wish fulfilled whatever that wish is until you actually feel all the tones of reality, all the things that you would normally feel were it true.

Now, don't forget that moment. That moment is productive. And in its own good time, that moment will appear in this world properly clothed as an objective fact. If it takes the whole vast world to aid its birth, it will take the whole vast world. If it takes an army of men to bring it to pass, an army of men. It doesn't really matter. You don't have to guide it. All you have to do is simply do it. And then let it alone as you would put a seed into the ground, confident that it will grow. Well, so you simply drop this, knowing what you did so that you aren't surprised when it happens in your world. So you want to be a man of wealth; all right assume that you're a man of wealth.

Not that it has any purpose in this world other than that you desired it. Because the man of wealth and the poor man are the same being. The poor state, the wealthy state are only states. The man who occupies the poor state is an individual that never ceases to be that individual. But if he falls into the state of poverty, well then you call him a poor man. But he doesn't differ from the man who falls into the state of wealth. For the man in the state of wealth; he's not any better; he has money, lots of money if he's a fabulously wealthy person. But that doesn't put him in a spiritual sense beyond the man that is poor.

But the man that is poor doesn't know he could get out of the state of poverty. All these are states, infinite states and man blindly falls into states. If he knows they're only states and he dislikes the state he's in, he'll get out of that state by now planting one of these moments, these heavenly moments by assuming that I am now secure.

The Wish Fulfilled

So, we are told: "All things are possible to God." Then we are told: "All things are possible to him who believes." So, the 19th chapter of Matthew tells us, "With God all things are possible." The 9th chapter of Mark tells us: "All things are possible to him who believes;" so he equates God with the man who can believe. You can't get away from that equation. If all things are possible to God and all things are possible to the one who believes, then he equates the one-who-believes with God.

No, I know the difference between thinking from my wish fulfilled and thinking of it. I am always thinking from where I am, and of where I am not. Right now, I am thinking from this room, and of my home, where my wife is now. But this room is more real now than where she is because I am thinking from here, and I am thinking of there. The secret is thinking from.

When you enter into a state and think from it, you give it all the tones of reality, you give it all the tones of reality, you give it all the sensory vividness that you can muster; and then when you open your eyes and you break the spell, you think, "Now, what have I done?" That was all imagination, the world would say. That's all it need be, for imagination is God! You set in motion a reality; and you do not have, now, to devise the means which will be employed to take you from where you are physically to where you are in imagination. So listen to the words carefully:

"And now I go to prepare a place for you; and when I go and prepare a place for you, I will come again and take you to my Self, that where I AM, there ye shall be also."

He is speaking to this "garment." This garment can't go. You sit it on a chair, put it on a bed, throw it on the floor; but He . . the Inner Man . . can be any place in this world; and viewing the world from where He is in imagination, which is Reality, He returns to the "ferment" that He left behind and takes it to Himself. So, I will return, having gone and prepared the place, . . I'll return and take you to myself, that where I AM . . Where? . . in consciousness, in my imagination . . which is the only Reality, there ye shall be also.

The Wish Fulfilled

Men go to church and pray to a god who does not exist, when the only God makes man alive, for man could not breathe, were God not housed within him. So when you find God, trust him implicitly; but let me warn you: He will not accept your orders! Only as you imagine the wish fulfilled, will He act upon it.

Tonight, as you put your head on that pillow, snuggle into the mood of the wish fulfilled in absolute confidence, and trust that God has ways and means your surface mind knows not of. I urge you to believe me, that you also may say with Paul: "I know whom I have believed." You will not fail, when you find the Lord your God, who is your own wonderful human imagination. You will learn to trust him completely. Knowing there is no need to help God by devising the means to fulfill your desire, you will move under compulsion, when the time for its fulfillment appears.

The Wish Fulfilled

I tell you, God is Love. He's Infinite Love. And He willingly gives everything if you come into His presence; and she knew anyone who got through that little door, that that one could receive anything that he voiced, because He would have voiced it and His words could not return unto Him void; they had to be accomplished. No matter what He sent them on, they had to fulfill the purpose for which He sent them.

And so, you need money? No, you don't. I share with you what I have discovered. All you need is to assume the feeling of the wish fulfilled. That's all that you need to do, because He is within you. Though asleep, He still grants the wish, for that is His Law. Assume the feeling of the wish fulfilled. Though reason denies it, though your senses deny it, don't waiver in that assumption. You assume it. Persist in the assumption, and that assumption will harden into reality, if you call reality these concrete things in the world. But really, these are the shadows. The reality was the invisible state that projected itself into what we can the "reality"; but the real Reality was invisible. Have faith. Have confidence in that invisible state. Assume it, "wear" it; it will externalize itself.

The Wish Fulfilled

Now we are told in the first book of Corinthians, the 15th chapter, that the "Second Man" is the Lord from Heaven, So, the second one who is mentioned in Genesis as Jacob, who became Israel as he wrestled successfully with the Lord, . . his name was changed from Jacob to Israel; he is that "Second Man." He came second; Esau came first. Well, this [indicating the body] is the "Esau"; and it's limited to its senses.

It can only accept as true what the senses dictate . . what reason allows. But there is something outside . . far beyond this, which is the "Second Man," and he is the Lord from Heaven. He is called in Scripture the Lord Jesus Christ.

So I stand here. I only accept as real what my senses now dictate . . the room; but I don't want to be here. Is there something in me that could dominate this little man that insists that this is the only reality? Well, certainly! It's my own wonderful human imagination!

Can I, while standing here, assume that I am elsewhere and see the world from that elsewhere-ness, and "see" it as I am now seeing this from this platform? I can do it. Well, if I do it, what would happen? I'll go there. Man, not knowing that, he is tied to his little body "Esau" morning, noon and night. He never gets away from it. But these rivals within man . . the second one eventually will become superior.

They are rival races from their birth; yet that younger one is destined to be the master; and the younger, which is the second, is the Lord from Heaven. And he will actually dominate when he comes awake within this wonderful story that is Scripture. And that second one is your own wonderful human imagination. So, I will stand here, and reason denies it, my senses deny it; my pocketbook will not allow it, and my time will not allow it, but I want to go elsewhere. Everything in this world tells me I can't go. Well, where would I go? I know exactly where I would go. Well now, let me in my imagination go. I don't travel; I bring "there" here, and "here" vanishes. I take "there" and make it "here"; and I take "then" and make it "now" And with my eyes closed to this world, I simply envelop myself in my wish fulfilled, and see the world as I would see it if it were physically true. And when it seems to take on all the tones of reality and all the sensory vividness of reality, then I open my eyes; and this world returns. That's what we are told in the Book of Genesis. Esau came back from the hunt, and as he came back Jacob vanished; but his father Isaac said, "Even though he deceived me into believing he was you, I cannot take away my blessing. I gave him my blessing. I gave him your birthright. I cannot take it back. I gave him the right of birth to come into this world and be as real as you seemingly are. So, now you must vanish, and he must take it even though he deceived me."

It was a self-deception. I deceived myself into believing that I am what one moment before reason denied and my senses denied. Try it! And if it proves itself in performance, does it really matter what the world thinks?

You see, we are dealing with the most fantastic mystery in the world, . . the mystery of imagining. That's what Fawcett said: "The secret of imagining is the greatest of all problems, to the solution of which every man should aspire, for supreme power, supreme wisdom, supreme delight lie in the far-off solution of this mystery," [from "The Zermatt Dialogues"] . . because you are actually solving the problem of God. If you can solve the problem of imagining, you are solving the problem of God!

The Wish Fulfilled

So tonight, if you are unemployed or threatened, may I tell you, don't despair. If you can't find a job, don't despair. If you want to be happily married and there seems to be no one in this world, whether you be male or female . . may I tell you, everyone is looking for the companion of his life or her life in this world. Assume that you have found him. Sleep as though it were true. Share it with your friends who have rejoiced with you, because it is true, and in a way that no one knows, out of the blue, she or he will come into your life, and it will be perfect.

I'm telling you from my own personal experience. That's why I can stand before you and say what I do. No one was more involved than the speaker when I found one that I said, "I've got to have her," but no one was more involved. And I simply slept as though it were true, and I can't tell you in detail what happened. The most mysterious things happened to make it possible in my world.

It is almost embarrassing to talk about it from the platform. I have talked about it, and those who were present criticized me unmercifully for having told the story, but I didn't tell it to brag. I told it to explain how the law works.

It works! You do not have to go out and devise the means to the end. Having assumed the end, the end will devise the means . . a series of incidents across which you will move. You will move across some bridge of incidents leading from where you have assumed the state to the fulfillment of it, because you go to the end, dwelling in the end. Then some strange thing happens in the world, and this bridge appears. You walk across the bridge of incidents leading up to the end.

Here recently . . when I say recently . . 1949, one of our great scientists discovered a certain principle in physics, and these are his words, not my words, but long before he discovered it and told it in this strange way, I told him, to the criticism of those who heard what I was saying. They said, "The man is insane."

I said, I can go in time into a state that is not yet realized, and I can live in that state as though it were true, and then I can return to this state that I have shut out for a moment, and then, in a way that I do not know, I move forward across a series of events leading up to the fulfillment of that state.

And a man in Milwaukee . . he was the head of this chemical department of a huge, huge organization . . Allis Chalmers. He was their great physicist, where they sent in all kinds of samples of water from all over the world for his analysis, to explain why they were getting sediment on the huge, big turbines that they were making. And so, he analyzed the water and then sent back his analysis of the water, because water picks up the little sediments across the land that it flows over. And so, if they bring certain things . . well, it cakes within the thing, so he tries to explain why.

So, when I said what I have just told you, he said, "It can't be done. We have a law in science, which we call entropy. Entropy is: "you cannot change the past; that the past is unalterable. Man is moving forward in time with an unalterable past." I said, "You can change the past. Man can revise the past, and change it as though it never happened. The day will come, everyone is going to change the entire past, and simply revise it." He said, "It can't be done. I am a scientist. I am the leader in my profession."

Well, he was big enough to send me a copy of that which came out in the Science Bulletin about two months after I left Milwaukee, and this is what the scientists said . . he had just been given the Nobel Prize for what he wrote in 1949. His name is Dr. Richard Feynman, now Professor of Physics at Cal-Tech. And in this magazine he wrote, months after I told the story in Milwaukee, and he said, discussing a little particle . . an atomic particle known as a positron: He said, "The positron starts from where it hasn't been, and it moves to where it was a moment before; arriving there, it is bounced so hard, its time sense is reversed, and it moves back to where it hasn't been." Now that is Professor Feynman of Cal-Tech.

I said, I go forward in time to where I have not yet visited physically, and I simply enclose myself in the feeling of the wish fulfilled. I haven't yet realized it physically, but I go forward in my mind's eye, in my imagination, into the state, and I talk with my friends from the wish fulfilled as though it were true. Then I open my eyes and I am startled to find that I am sitting in a chair where I was a moment before. And what I have just done is denied by my senses, but strangely enough, the whole vast world reshuffles itself and forms a bridge of incidents, across which I move to the fulfillment of that state where I have been. So, he said, "It starts from where it hasn't been, and it moves to where it was an instant ago. Arriving there, it is bounced so hard that its time sense is reversed, and then it travels back to where it hasn't been."

Well, I knew that mystically. I am not a scientist. I could not explain it. The little positron does this as he described it back in 1949. And for that, last year he was given the Nobel Prize. They waited all these years to confirm it, and it has been confirmed now photographically in all the chambers that they could actually test, and the man was right. But I was right before that! But I had no little particle to prove it. I only know what I did.

I simply would put myself in a state, and I would see the world as I would see it if it were true. I looked, and I saw it, and my friends smiling with me because they were happy that I achieved what I said I would achieve. And so, they were smiling with me. And then I opened my eyes, and my friends aren't present. I am back in my room, and it's the same old room, the same limitations, the same everything. But then, in a way I did not know, this little bridge of incidents was built, and I went forward to fulfill what I had done.

I went forward and I did what I wanted to do. And then I started from where I had not been physically, and sped back to where I was physically; and then I was bounced . . shocked . . that it wasn't true. I was bounced so hard that I then turned around in my time sense and moved back to fulfill where I had been in my imagination.

Now, the issue is October the 15th. It's called the Science Letter. You can get it in the Library. It's by Richard Feynman . . October the 15th, 1949. And this happened to me in the month of May in the City of Milwaukee. And when it came out to him, because he subscribes to the Science Letter, he sent it to me, and I got it sometime around December of that year; but I said it to him back in May of that year. I didn't get the Nobel Prize. They would have called me mad . . completely mad.

May I tell you: "There are states of consciousness in which all visionary men are accounted mad men" [Blake, from "The Laocoon"]. And I've been accounted a mad man since a child, because I've been seeing things that I could not explain. I didn't have the education to explain these things that I have seen, but I knew they worked. I only knew that it worked. I would try it, and it worked.

If there is evidence for a thing, does it really matter what the world thinks about it, if there is evidence for it? Well, I had the evidence for it, but I could not explain it scientifically. I only knew that it worked.

So, I tell you, all things are possible to him who believes, and that One is equal to God. Only the limitation is placed upon God-as-man, because, "With God all things are possible," without restriction. To imagine from the Divine Imagining state, it's automatic . . it's done. But when God limits Himself to man and comes down to the limit of man, then He imposes upon Himself, called man, belief. So, "Without faith," we are told, "it is impossible to please Him; and he who would come to God must first believe that God exists, and He rewards those who seek Him."

The Wish Fulfilled

I know this much: if you believe to the point of acceptance, life will be marvelous for you, perfectly wonderful for this is the one secret in the world that everyone should aspire to solve, for God is that pure imaging in ourselves. He underlies all of our faculties including our perception, but he streams into our surface mind least disguised in the form of productive fantasy. I sit here and have a daydream. Well, that's God in action, but then someone breaks it and I forget it. I didn't occupy it; I simply had a daydream but without occupancy. That's one of the greatest fallacies of the world, 'perpetual construction'. It's a daydream, deferred occupancy. I don't occupy it, I don't go in and possess it and make it mine.

If I, in my Imagination, could go right in and possess it and make it mine...If I, in my Imagination, could go right in and possess it and clothe myself with the feeling of the wish fulfilled, actually clothe myself with it by assuming that it's done now, until I feel natural in that assumption and that assumption though at the moment denied by my senses, if persisted in will harden into fact. [a statement made by Anthony Eden at the Guild Hall when he was Prime Minister of England]. So, this is our great secret concerning imagining.

If you doubt it tonight, I would only ask you not to deny it to the point of not trying it, but hold it in abeyance and try it now. Just try it, even if you want to disprove it. I tell you, you will not disprove it. You will in the attempt to disprove it, prove it. And then slowly you will come to completely accept it and then you will walk in the company of God.

You won't have to wait for Sunday morning to meet him in a church or any time of day. No matter where you are, you could be standing in a bar enjoying a drink, having fun at a dance and you are in the company of God. It makes no difference where you are once you know God and God is your own wonderful human Imagination and you'll become extremely discriminating because you'll know you can't entertain these ideas with complete acceptance of them and not reap them in your world.

The Wish Fulfilled

Creation is finished and you have free will to choose the state you will occupy. Therefore, it is important to determine the ideas from which you think. Any concept that is accepted as true will externalize itself in your outer world. Choice of what you will focus your attention upon is the only free will that you can exercise. Once a thought is accepted and charged with feeling, the creative power within proceeds to externalize it. Whether your assumptions are conscious or unconscious, they direct all action to their fulfillment. It is a delusion that, other than assuming the feeling of the wish fulfilled, you can do anything to aid its realization. Your own wonderful human imagination determines the means it will use to bring your assumptions to fruition.

Each of us is subject to a sea of ideas. We listen to the radio, watch the news on television, or hear some gossip. If what we observe calls forth an emotion, we have reacted and, thereby, planted a seed which will sprout at some future time. Thoughts do not recede into the past. Rather, they advance into the future to confront us so that we may see that which we have planted, either wisely or unwisely.

It is a worthwhile exercise to awake in the morning and imagine yourself at the end of your day, having accomplished all that you wanted and feeling happy and contented. If there is a situation that you will encounter later in the day that is of concern to you, spend a few moments imagining the outcome you wish to experience. These imaginal activities will now advance into your future to reveal the harvest you so wisely planted.

The Wish Fulfilled

All of us are mentally speaking within ourselves every waking moment. Our inner conversations must match the wish fulfilled if we would realize our desire. If our desire is for a better job and we imagine ourselves being congratulated because we are gainfully employed in a wonderful position, we must also make our inner conversations conform to that end. We must be certain that we are not saying within ourselves something like, "That boss of mine doesn't believe in promoting people;" or "It would be difficult to find any job at my age, never mind a better one," or similar statements that would imply that we do not have that which we desire. We must persist in the feeling of our imaginal act by making our mental conversations conform to what we would say had we already realized our aim.

If, for instance, we wished to own a new car, we could imagine a new car parked in our garage or imagine ourselves driving it, or imagine our friends admiring it. We must then make our inner conversations reflect the type of conversations we would engage in were we really the owner of a new car. Our conversations could consist of discussing our new car with friends such as telling them of the wonderful fuel mileage we are receiving, or hearing our friends tell us how much they enjoy riding in our new car, etc.

Our inner conversations are just as creative as our deliberate imagining of the wish fulfilled. In fact, if they are of the opposite nature, they can negate what we have imagined. You must watch what you are saying internally to make sure that these conversations coincide with your wish fulfilled. If you become aware that these inner talks contradict what you would like to achieve, revise them so that they follow along the track that would indicate that you already have what you desire or are already the person you wish to be.

The Wish Fulfilled

Your present world reflects the sum total of all that you believe to be true of yourself and others. That which you imagine yourself to be today goes forward and will confront you in the future. If you have forgotten your imaginal activities of the past, that which you see appearing in your world indicates the kind of seeds you have previously sown.

Assuming the feeling of your wish fulfilled is using your imagination creatively to bring into your world that which you desire to experience. You can use the art of revision to change the effects of prior thoughts and beliefs.

If, for instance, you had gone to an interview for a job you truly wanted but later learned that someone else was hired, you can revise that news to make it conform to what you wish you had heard. If you react by feeling depressed or assume any other negative attitude, you will then experience the same type of rejection in the future. Your reactions, whether positive or negative, are creative of future circumstances. In your imagination, you can hear words congratulating you on getting a wonderful new job. That imaginal act now goes forward and you will encounter this pleasant experience in the future.

As you review your day, it is important to revise each negative reaction so that you can remember it as what you wished had happened rather than storing that memory as it did occur. What you think of with feeling or emotion is an actual fact. That which you experience in the physical world is merely a shadow, reflecting the reality of your imaginal activity. Therefore, when you revise a conversation, an unhappy experience, or a quality about yourself, you are literally experiencing it in reality (your consciousness). The outer world is a delayed reflection of the inner and is confined to a dimension of space where events occur in a time sequence. Revision, then, literally changes the past. It replaces what occurred in the outer world with the revised version. The revised scene then gives off its effect by going forth to change future events.

Dwelling on past irritations or hurts perpetuates them and creates a vicious circle that serves to confirm these negative emotions. The circle can be broken by starting now to revise anything that you no longer wish to sustain in your world. By revising the past, you rid yourself of any effect it may have on your future. Revision is truly the key, which can be used to unlock the doors that have kept you trapped in a particular state. "Be ye transformed by the renewing of your mind."

The Wish Fulfilled

As Shakespeare said, "All the world's a stage and all the men and women merely players. They have their exits and their entrances... and each man in his time plays many parts." This world, which seems so real, is as much a dream as the dreams we encounter while asleep. Our waking dream seems so real because it has continuity while our dreams at night appear to be random sequences, taking place in unfamiliar surroundings and situations.

God is the dreamer, dreaming the play into existence, and God plays all the parts. Everyone who appears in your world is God playing that part for you, the author. "No man comes unto me, save I call him." Each of us is writing his or her own script. If you are dissatisfied with the play, it is up to you to rewrite the script to make it conform to your idea of what the play should be. You cannot demand that the actors in your play change the character they are portraying. All changes must take place in the mind of the author.

If there is someone in your world who is the source of annoyance or irritation to you, that person has no choice but to play the part called for in your script. There is nothing you can do on the outside to bring about changes in another. You can use the art of revision to change a line of dialogue, to replace a certain character with another, and to write happy endings to the sub-plots of the play.

When you begin to view this waking dream objectively, you will be able to verify that you have been the author of both the pleasant and unhappy acts in your play. You can radically change the play by using your imagination creatively, by assuming your wish fulfilled.

You can change the script on a daily basis by revising the scene that did not please you. The character who disturbed you today will not do so tomorrow if you write the dialogue you wish to hear and alter that role in your imagination.

When you awaken to know that you are God, the Father and author of this magnificent play, you will understand that: “each man in his time plays many parts.”

The Wish Fulfilled

What should be done after we have imagined our wish fulfilled? Nothing. You think you can do something, you want to do something, but actually you can do nothing to bring it about. God, our own wonderful human imagination, knows what things are necessary to bring about our desires. It is only necessary to go to the end, to live in the end. "My ways are past finding out." "My ways are higher than your ways." If we trust our imagination, it will "accomplish all that we ask of it." Imagination can do all things . . have faith in it, and nothing shall be impossible to you.

The Wish Fulfilled

I urge you to dream nobly. Although your dream may seem impossible, invite it into your consciousness by feeling it is real. Wear this feeling as you would a suit of clothes, and persist until the feeling takes on the tones of reality. Do that, and in a way no one knows, your desire will appear as an eruption of your continuous thought.

Your desire started in motion when you wore it. Its appearance is simply a hidden continuity which came to the surface. Dwell upon a thought, and you will realize that it is not original. That the thought itself is complete and therefore every thought is Divine plagiarism!

Enter a mood and watch the thoughts that come to you while there. If you want to be known, get into the mood by feeling recognized as you move about. Then as the feeling becomes familiar you will be amazed how things will reshuffle themselves and you will get the publicity you desire. It may not be very flattering, but if you really want to be known, you will be.

"Whatever you desire, believe you have received it and you will." Knowing what you want, assume you have it and let no one divert you. Do your father's will, believing in the feeling of your wish fulfilled. Try it, for this simple principle will not fail you. But remember: you are its power, as it does not operate itself. I can tell you how to move into another state, but you must move into it. No one can do it for you. You see, states are permanent and it is up to you to get out of the state you are now in if it is undesirable to you.

The Wish Fulfilled

Take the challenge of scripture: "Whatever you desire, believe you have received it and you will." Dare to believe you have what reason and your senses deny. Persist in your assumption and it will harden into fact. Try it and see! And remember: the Father who became you is speaking to you through the medium of dream and revealing himself in vision, for this world is His play!

One day you will leave this play, knowing you are God the Father who conceived it all. Beginning as the one God, we fell as the gods. But we will return to the one God, for it takes all of us to form the Lord. "Hear O Israel, the Lord our God, is one Lord."

Take the challenge of scripture and assume the feeling of the wish fulfilled . . not only for yourself, but for your family and friends. When you imagine for another, you are really giving it to yourself, as there is no other. The whole vast world is only yourself pushed out.

The Wish Fulfilled

Prayer is the elevation of the mind to that which we seek.

The very first word of correction is always "arise."

Always lift the mind to that which we seek. This is easily done by assuming the feeling of the wish fulfilled. How would you feel if your prayer were answered? Well, assume that feeling until you experience in imagination what you would experience in reality, if your prayer were answered.

Prayer means getting into action mentally. It means holding the attention upon the idea of the wish fulfilled until it fills the mind and crowds all other ideas out of the consciousness.

This statement that prayer means getting into action mentally and holding the attention upon the idea of the wish fulfilled until it fills the mind and crowds all other ideas out of the consciousness, does not mean that prayer is a mental effort, an act of will.

On the contrary, prayer is to be contrasted with an act of will. Prayer is a surrender. It means abandoning oneself to the feeling of the wish fulfilled.

If prayer brings no response, there is something wrong with the prayer and the fault lies generally in too much effort.

Serious confusion arises insofar as men identify the state of prayer with an act of will, instead of contrasting it with an act of will. The sovereign rule is to make no effort, and if this is observed, you will intuitively fall into the right attitude.

Creativeness is not an act of will, but a deeper receptiveness, a keener susceptibility. The acceptance of the end . . the acceptance of the answered prayer . . finds the means for its realization.

Feel yourself into the state of the answered prayer until the state fills the mind and crowds all other states out of your consciousness. What we must work for is not the development of the will, but the education of the imagination and the steadying of attention.

Prayer succeeds by avoiding conflict. Prayer is, above all things, easy. Its greatest enemy is effort. The mighty surrenders itself fully only to that which is most gentle. The wealth of Heaven may not be seized by a strong will, but surrenders itself, a free gift, to the God. . spent moment. Along the lines of least resistance travel spiritual as well as physical forces.

We must act on the assumption that we already possess that which we desire, for all that we desire is already present within us. It only waits to be claimed. That it must be claimed is a necessary condition by which we realize our desires.

Our prayers are answered if we assume the feeling of the wish fulfilled and continue in that assumption.

The Wish Fulfilled

The necessity of persistence in prayer is shown us in the Bible.

"Which of you," asked Jesus,

"shall go unto him at midnight, and say unto him: Friend, lend me three loaves; for a friend of mine is come to me from a journey, and I have nothing to set before him":

and he from within shall answer and say,

'Trouble me not; the door is now shut and my children are with me in bed; I cannot rise and give thee.' I say unto you, though he will not rise and give him because he is his friend, yet because of his importunity he will arise and give as many as he needeth."

The word translated as "importunity" means, literally, shameless impudence. We must persist until we succeed in imagining ourselves into the situation of the answered prayer.

The secret of success is found in the word "perseverance." The soul imagining itself into the act, takes on the results of the act. Not imagining itself into the act, it is ever free from the result.

Experience in imagination, what you would experience in reality were you already what you want to be, and you will take on the result of that act. Do not experience in imagination what you want to experience in reality and you will ever be free of the result.

"When ye pray, believe that ye receive, and ye shall receive."

One must persist until he reaches his friend on a higher level of consciousness. He must persist until his feeling of the wish fulfilled has all the sensory vividness of reality.

Prayer is a controlled waking dream. If we are to pray successfully, we must steady our attention to observe the world as it would be seen by us were our prayer answered.

Steadying attention makes no call upon any special faculty, but it does demand control of imagination. We must extend our senses . . observe our changed relationship to our world and trust this observation. The new world is not there to grasp, but to sense, to touch.

The best way to observe it is to be intensely aware of it. In other words, we can, by listening as though we heard and by looking as though we saw, actually hear voices and see scenes from within ourselves that are otherwise not audible or visible.

With our attention focused on the state desired, the outer world crumbles and then the world, like music, by a new setting, turns all its discords into harmonies.

Life is not a struggle but a surrender.

Our prayers are answered by the powers we invoke not by those we exert.

So long as the eyes take notice, the soul is blind . . for the world that moves us is the one we imagine, not the world round about us.

We must yield our whole being to the feeling of being the noble one we want to be. If anything is kept back, the prayer is vain. We often are deprived of our high goal by our effort to possess it.

We are called upon to act on the assumption that we already are the man we would be. If we do this without effort . . experiencing in imagination what we would experience in the flesh had we realized our goal, we shall find that we do, indeed, possess it.

The healing touch is in our attitude.

We need change nothing but our attitude towards it. Assume a virtue if you have it not, assume the feeling of your wish fulfilled.

"Pray for my soul; more things are wrought by prayer than this world dreams of."

The Wish Fulfilled

Meditation, like sleep, is an entrance into the subconscious.

"When you pray, enter into your closet, and when you have shut your door, pray to your Father which is in secret and your Father which is in secret shall reward you openly."

Meditation is an illusion of sleep which diminishes the impression of the outer world and renders the mind more receptive to suggestion from within.

The mind in meditation is in a state of relaxation akin to the feeling attained just before dropping off to sleep. This state is beautifully described by the poet, Keats, in his "Ode To A Nightingale. It is said that as the poet sat in the garden and listened to the nightingale, he fell into a state which he described as

"A drowsy numbness pains my senses as though of hemlock I had drunk."

Then after singing his ode to the nightingale,

Keats asked himself this question,

"Was it a vision or a waking dream?

Fled is the music; do I wake or sleep?"

Those are the words of one who has seen something with such vividness or reality that he wonders whether the evidence of his physical eyes can now be believed.

Any kind of meditation in which we withdraw into ourselves, without making too much effort to think, is an outcropping of the subconscious.

Think of the subconscious as a tide which ebbs and flows. In sleep, it is a flood tide, while at moments of full wakefulness, the tide is at its lowest ebb.

Between these two extremes are any number of intermediary levels.

When we are drowsy, dreamy, lulled in gentle reverie, the tide is high. The more wakeful and alert we become, the lower the tide sinks.

The highest tide compatible with the conscious direction of our thoughts occurs just before we fall asleep and just after we wake.

An easy way to create this passive state is to relax in a comfortable chair or on a bed. Close your eyes and imagine that you are sleepy, so sleepy, so very sleepy. Act precisely as though you were going to take a siesta. In so doing, you allow the subconscious tide to rise to sufficient height to make your particular assumption effective.

When you first attempt this, you may find that all sorts of counter thoughts try to distract you, but if you persist, you will achieve a passive state.

When this passive state is reached, think only on "things of good report" . . imagine that you are now expressing your highest ideal, not how you will express it, but simply feel here and now, that you are the noble one you desire to be.

You are it now.

Call your high ideal into being by imagining and feeling you are it now.

I think all happiness depends on the energy to assume the feeling of the wish fulfilled, to assume the mask of some other, more perfect life. If we cannot imagine ourselves different from what we are and try to assume that second more desirable self, we cannot impose a discipline upon ourselves, though we may accept discipline from others.

Meditation is an activity of the soul; it is an active virtue; and an active virtue, as distinguished from passive acceptance of a code, is theatrical. It is dramatic; it is the wearing of a mask.

As your goal is accepted, you become totally indifferent to possible failure, for acceptance of the end wills the means to the end.

When you emerge from the moment of meditation it is as though you were shown the happy end of a play in which you are the principal actor. Having witnessed the end in your meditation, regardless of any anticlimactic state you encounter, you remain calm and secure in the knowledge that the end has been perfectly defined.

Creation is finished and what we call creativeness is really only a deeper receptiveness or keener susceptibility on our part, and this receptiveness is

"Not by might, nor by power, but by my spirit, saith the Lord of Hosts."

Through meditation, we awaken within ourselves a center of light, which will be to us a pillar of cloud by day and a pillar of fire by night.

The Wish Fulfilled

Men believe in the reality of the external world because they do not know how to focus and condense their powers to penetrate its thin crust.

Strangely enough, it is not difficult to penetrate this view of the senses.

To remove the veil of the senses, we do not employ great effort; the objective world vanishes as we turn our attention from it.

We have only to concentrate on the state desired to mentally see it; but to give reality to it so that it will become an objective fact, we must focus our attention upon the desired state until it has all the sensory vividness and feeling of reality.

When, through concentrated attention, our desire appears to possess the distinctness and feeling of reality; when the form of thought is as vivid as the form of nature, we have given it the right to become a visible fact in our lives.

Each man must find the means best suited to his nature to control his attention and concentrate it on the desired state.

I find for myself the best state to be one of meditation, a relaxed state akin to sleep, but a state in which I am still consciously in control of my imagination and capable of fixing my attention on a mental object.

If it is difficult to control the direction of your attention while in this state akin to sleep, you may find gazing fixedly into an object very helpful. Do not look at its surface, but rather into and beyond any plain object such as a wall, a carpet or any object which possesses depth. Arrange it to return as little reflection as possible. Imagine, then, that in this depth you are seeing and hearing what you want to see and hear until your attention is exclusively occupied by the imagined state.

At the end of your meditation, when you awake from your controlled waking dream you feel as though you had returned from a great distance.

The visible world which you had shut out, returns to consciousness and, by its very presence, informs you that you have been self-deceived into believing that the object of your contemplation was real; but if you remain faithful to your vision this sustained mental attitude will give reality to your visions and they will become visible concrete facts in your world.

Define your highest ideal and concentrate your attention upon this ideal until you identify yourself with it. Assume the feeling of being it, the feeling that would be yours were you now embodying it in your world.

This assumption, though now denied by your senses,

"if persisted in",

will become a fact in your world. You will know when you have succeeded in fixing the desired state in consciousness simply by looking mentally at the people you know.

This is a wonderful check on yourself, as your mental conversations are more revealing than your physical conversations are. If, in your mental conversations with others, you talk with them as you formerly did, then you have not changed your concept of self, for all changes of concepts of self result in a changed relationship to the world.

Remember what was said earlier,

"What you see when you look at something depends not so much on what is there as on the assumption you make when you look."

Therefore, the assumption of the wish fulfilled should make you see the world mentally as you would physically were your assumption a physical fact.

The spiritual man speaks to the natural man through the language of desire. The key to progress in life and to the fulfillment of dreams lies in the ready obedience to the voice. Unhesitating obedience to its voice is an immediate assumption of the wish fulfilled.

To desire a state is to have it.

As Pascal said,

"You would not have sought me had you not already found me."

Man, by assuming the feeling of the wish fulfilled and then living and acting on this conviction changes his future in harmony with his assumption.

To "change his future" is the inalienable right of freedom loving individuals. There would be no progress in the world were it not for the divine discontent in man which urges him on to higher and higher levels of consciousness.

The Wish Fulfilled

So make your dream and live in it and it will come true. We are told that as the sower sowed, the seed fell on four kinds of soil. The first is not prepared; it is the highway, and no seed took root. These are those who will not listen. Then you will find one who will take this teaching, but it falls on stony ground. They get something new but there is no root. The first thing they say is: "Oh, it would have happened anyway!" The third fell among the "thorns and thistles." It grows deeper than the one on the rock, but they really believe that it is only with money they can get things and so the teaching was choked by the thorns of their unbelief.

Then there is the well-prepared ground, and it roots deeply and produces fifty and a hundred been prepared for your education and that it is all interwoven in the labyrinthine ways of your own mind. And then you learn to walk in the feeling of your wish fulfilled, and you can create states from this heavenly alphabet of God, and then we find how the entire Bible story is a true story as seen through the eyes of those who wrote it. It is the history of the soul of man and some day you will know it is taking place in you, and then it moves rapidly and you will understand the vision you did not understand before. Then you can say: "The whole Book spoke of me!"

The Wish Fulfilled

Take what you know of this law, and use it towards your own personal good fortune in the world of Caesar. It's simple. Go to the end and assume the feeling of the wish fulfilled. Don't ask anyone to help you. Ask no one if it is right. If you like it, assume you have it. Remain faithful to your assumption, and that Being who is going to erupt in you will take you to that end. If you find yourself moving from your fulfilled desire, go back to it, and once more assume the feeling of the wish fulfilled. Do this and your assumption will harden into fact.

The Wish Fulfilled

There was a lady in San Francisco. She said, "My brother". . and she said to me, "I think he's innocent, but I do not know the facts of the case; but he was given six months at hard labor. He is in the Army. And I don't think my brother should get six months' hard labor in the Army."

I said, "You want him out?"

She said, "Certainly I do."

I said, "I tell you what. You may try it, so that you may give all praise to yourself and not to me. You do it."

"Well, what must I do?"
"If he was out, would he come home?"

"Oh, yes, he'd come straight to my place."

"All right. And if he came to your place, what would you do?"

"Well," she said, "I would throw my arms around him and kiss him, feel him."

I said, "All right, do that. When you go home tonight sit where you would normally sit, and just imagine that your brother is there and that you have thrown your arms around him and you are holding him and hugging him, and kissing him."

The next Sunday morning in my meeting in San Francisco, that woman could rise and tell this story. She said, "I went home, and I imagined I heard the doorbell ring; and the doorbell is downstairs. I have to run down one flight of stairs to answer that door. So, I heard it ring and I ran downstairs, and I flung the doors open, and here stood my brother. I went back upstairs. There was no brother, but I did it so vividly that it was almost like a disappointment that I didn't actually see him standing there, because it seemed so real to me."

Well, a few days later she was sitting upstairs and the doorbell rang. She said, "I almost broke my neck to get downstairs. I knew what was going to happen." As she threw the door open, here was her brother!

She stood up in the audience and told that story to the thousand who were present that Sunday morning. They all saw her. No one, I presume, would go and verify it; I trusted her implicitly. If she lied to me, then it's entirely up to her; but I am convinced the whole thing was true.

I don't check on you. I believe you when you tell me that it happened. But the thing is to practice. We are the operant power. And the Flood is on. Let no one tell you the Flood is over. And the Flood is deeper and deeper, because we are more and more inclined for facts . . the “facts of life.” Do you want the facts? Well, you had better make the prison walls all the thicker. But learn how to penetrate the facts.

As you penetrate the facts, you must go to a certain objective beyond the fact. What do you want now? Well then, you go into the state of the wish fulfilled. What is the state? You decide. You determine what you want in this world, and you go right into that state, and then ignore the facts.

Suppose the facts now still deny what you did. It doesn't matter. Let the facts remain; they will dissolve. They will all dissolve because you are going to remain faithful and you will occupy the state. No longer are you going to construct it and not occupy it. You are going to occupy the state. And as you occupy the state, it is going to work.

The Wish Fulfilled

Your assumption, though false in the sense that it is denied by your reasonable mind, if persisted in will harden into fact. You do not need to know the means that will be employed to bring your assumption to pass; all you are required to do is persist in your assumption and allow your own wonderful human imagination to give it to you.

All things are possible to your imagination. It's up to you to provide the necessary link between your assumption and its fulfillment. That link is faith. Having assumed your desire is fulfilled, your faith in that assumption will cause it to harden into fact. That is the law.

Test this law, and if you prove it in performance, it will not matter to you if it seems irrational to others. Tonight, leave this auditorium in the assumption that you are what you would like to be; and if tomorrow your assumption can be seen as fact by the world round about you, then you have found Christ, he who is within you as your hope of glory.

Man is forever coming up with fantastic ideas like going to the moon. At the time, the idea seemed impossible, yet in time man does go to the moon. So you see, nothing is impossible to God . . but nothing!

Simply name that which seems so impossible to you, then assume that you have it. Walk in the assumption it is now an objective fact and see how God works. I tell you, in a way that you do not know, and you could not possibly devise, you will be led across a bridge of incident to the fulfillment of that state. All you have to do is ignore the evidence of your outer senses and go about your own wonderful business assuming the feeling of the wish fulfilled. Your assumption, instead of receding into the past, will advance into the future and you will walk right into its fulfillment.

The Wish Fulfilled

One of the loveliest examples of an answered prayer I witnessed in my own living room. A very charming lady from out of town came to see me concerning prayer. As she had no one with whom to leave her eight-year old son, she brought him with her the time of our interview. Seemingly, he was engrossed in playing with a toy truck, but at the end of the interview with his mother he said,

"Mr. Neville, I know how to pray now. I know what I want . . a collie puppy . . and I can imagine I am hugging him every night on my bed."

His mother explained to him and to me the impossibilities of his prayer, the cost of the puppy, their confined home, even his inability to care for the dog properly.

The boy looked into his mother's eyes and simply said, "But, Mother, I know how to pray now." And he did. Two months later during a "Kindness to Animals Week" in his city, all the school children were required to write an essay on how they would love and care for a pet.

You have guessed the answer.

His essay, out of the five thousand submitted, won the prize, and that prize, presented by the mayor of the city to the lad . . was a collie puppy. The boy truly assumed the feeling of his wish fulfilled, hugging and loving his puppy every night.

The Wish Fulfilled

"If we know that He hears us in whatever we ask, we know we have obtained the request made of Him." Read that in the First Epistle of John, the 5th chapter, 15th verse. These are statements made by the Awakened Man. Therefore, if the prayer is not answered, you are praying to a wrong god. But if you know that the God to Whom you pray is your own wonderful human imagination, then instead of begging, you appropriate.

You appropriate the state; so I call it the subjective appropriation of the objective hope. What is my objective hope? Well, I appropriate it subjectively. I "go within" and I simply appropriate it. I simply assume the feeling of my wish fulfilled. I appropriate it; and if my wish fulfilled were true, how would I see the world in which I live? and then do everything to make me see it as I would see it if it were: see the people in my world as I would have to see them, and let them see me as they would be compelled to see me if what I am doing is an actual external fact. If they know me and I know them, and something happens in my life that becomes public knowledge, . . well, then, they would know it. Then let them see me as they would have to see me if it were true. So, the subjective appropriation of the objective hope is prayer. You don't beg any one. Don't ask anyone. You simply appropriate it. For, if He is in me, where would I go to ask Him?

The Wish Fulfilled

What I did in February took approximately seven months to mature. I did it . . consciously did it, not thinking for one moment . . I did it only to relax and to put myself into that mood because I was disappointed that the crowd did not come out and get my new book, "Your Faith Is Your Fortune," So, I tell you from experience, don't do it idly, because when you plant something, that is still coming into being. It is going to come into being and disturb your so-called conscious plans. It works that way. So, I do know that when it comes back into this world, it doesn't really matter. I stand here just perfectly simply now and do something in my mind's eye and give it sensory vividness and give it the tones of reality, and then I open my eyes, and this shocks me, because this tells me that what I just did was self-deception. You deceive yourself. It is all in your imagination. But I know now that my imagination is the only reality; that this world is still the world of imagination, and that all the things that I see as an objective fact in my world . . they are all "pushed out" because of my imagined acts.

To try to change circumstances before I change my imaginal activity is to work against the very nature of things. It can't change of itself. It can only change as I change the imaginal activity. So, if I now actually know the man that I would like to be, though at the moment reason denies it and my senses deny it . . if I really know what I'd like to be so that I could write it out, name it, state it . . well, then, in my mind's eye assume that I am that man. And to prove that I am that man, look at my friends' faces, look at the people in my world and let them see me as they would have to see me if it were true. Then if I want to carry on a conversation with them, carry on the conversation from the premise of my wish fulfilled, and then have them say to me what they would have to say. And I say to them what I would say, were I such a man, and then see what happens. And you mold yourself into that being, for you are not discarding yourself. You do not jump off the bridge because you do not like yourself as you are; you simply remold yourself.

So, the vessel in the hand of the potter was spoiled, but he didn't discard the vessel. He reworked it into another vessel as it seemed good to the potter to do. And the potter was his own wonderful human imagination. And that is addressed in Scripture as God.

The Wish Fulfilled

So, this Power . . and there are in this audience tonight those who have tasted of the Power; there are those who have tasted, I hope, of the Wisdom, where you know you do nothing to make it so. It just is so because you are perfect. Therefore, you are told: "Be ye perfect, as your Father in Heaven is perfect." When that Perfection is yours, everything in the world is perfect.

No matter what happens to you and to those you love, you still cannot for one moment entertain the thought that God is cruel, even though you see what appears to be a horrible thing taking place in your most intimate world. Yet, you still maintain your conviction that God is Love. For, when you experience God as Infinite Love, not a thing in the world can turn you from that conviction. You know God is Love . . that's all there is to it, and you stand in the presence of the Ancient of Days, and you can't think of anything but love. And the Ancient of Days embraces you, and you fuse and become one body. You are the Ancient of Days. And then you are sent, and you do the job that you are sent to do. Then, as you are sent, you are the Word. "And His name shall be called the Word of God."

And you are told," My word that goes forth from my mouth shall not return unto me void, but it shall accomplish that which I purpose and prosper in the thing for which I sent it." It cannot come back void, so you will return to the Father, having accomplished the work that He gave you to do. And at that return, you are God Himself! You are the Father!

I'm not here to flatter you. I'm not here to change what you are doing now. If you feel that you have not completed the world of Caesar and you want something better in the world of Caesar . . a bigger home or more homes and more money, more fame, more recognition . . all right. If that's your hunger, may I tell you, you're entitled to it, and you can get it. You can get it by simply assuming the feeling of the wish fulfilled, and remaining faithful to that assumption. And if you remain faithful to that assumption, it will become a fact. He puts no limit on the power of belief . . none whatsoever.

"Whatsoever you desire, believe that you have received it, and you will." That is the promise made in the 11th chapter of the book of Mark.

It doesn't say if it's good for you or it is wrong, if you desire it. There is no restriction upon the limit . . upon the limit of belief . . none. So, if you know what you want, and you dare assume that you have it, and live as though you have it, and live in the end . . viewing the world from the end instead of thinking of the end, because God in becoming man does not think of man; He thinks from man. That's the secret.

The Wish Fulfilled

So, let us turn back and freshen up again this word which has been so abused, which now is your imagination, which people, without defining, call the "subconscious" as though it was some appendage. People go around speaking of "my subconscious mind", or "My unconscious mind", not knowing what they are referring to.

Well, this fabulous series of mental states is your imagination. And may I tell you it has form, it has structure, just as real as the visible objective world; that the inner world is a world of reality. Call it by any name. I call it my wonderful imagination, and it assumes the form of all that I accept and consent to as true. It actually assumes the form of the sum total of all of my beliefs, and my beliefs need not be true. They need not come near the truth. My beliefs could be prejudices; they could be superstitions. It doesn't care. It will take all the stripes of men and wear them. So it will assume the form of the sum total of all that man consents to in this world, and then mold the outer world in harmony with the inner arrangement of itself. Therefore, to change the outer world, I must modify or change, in some way alter, the structure of the inner or second man . . the second man being my imagination.

So I set myself to observe myself and to watch how my imagination works. And here is something that will interest you. I observe it always moves according to habit; that it is a being of habit, and so if I get into the habit of thinking the unlovely thoughts, it becomes very natural, so I listen only to that which is critical of another. I listen only to that which is not full of praise, that which judges harshly, and so according to habit it moves along these pathways.

Now, if I don't like the outer world, and I really believe it is caused by the structure of the inner or second man, I then must change his likeness, change his form, by observing how I react to all the unlovely, and how I am not interested in the praise of another, and then begin to feed my sheep, begin to change my thoughts, my feelings, my moods concerning others, and as I begin to change my reactions to people, I find I am changing the structure of the Son of God. And then I automatically produce corresponding changes in my outer world.

If you really like it, and you are bold enough to take it, I promise you a world that is undreamed of by our wise men for even sleep will no longer be the unconscious that it is to the majority of people in the world; that sleep becomes only a doorway into the world where this real you . . the second man . . really lives and moves and has its being. It is a dimensionally larger world, and you enter it quickly in meditation, or night after night in sleep, and you will find opportunities that would dwarf the wildest dream of men here.

So I ask you to really believe it, and try in the short interval of four weeks while we are here to so prove it that you can tell me of the things that have happened to you by putting into practice this Power of Awareness. Learn to become aware at any moment of time of your fulfilled desire. Assume the feeling of your wish fulfilled and learn to become intensely aware of the state fulfilled, that you may look upon your world and describe it relative to your fulfilled desire. And learn then to sustain that mood. You will find in time through the habitual motion of your inner you, after a little while, because it always travels according to habit, it will move through habit into the feeling of the wish fulfilled, and the moment it is a natural wearing to itself, it starts to change the outer world to reflect the inner change of your mind.

Now, I hope you will take it, but there is no power in the world that can compel you to take it. You are as free as the wind to take it or not to take it. If you would rather persist in the belief that your Savior lived years ago and died for you and through his death, external to yourself, you are saved; you are entitled to believe it.

As I told you earlier, because the inner you is molded in harmony with the sum total of all your beliefs, you will continue to have visible proof of the truth of that belief. For you will find millions believing with you, and you will believe that the numbers make it right, and so you will contribute to the whole vast traditions of men. If you want to come out and be apart and find your savior where you will only find Him, within yourself, by setting your imagination to observe itself, you must come to the same conclusion . . that this ultimate reality that men call God, that the Ancients defined as I AM, is your own wonderful consciousness and that IT in action, or the Son, or Christ Jesus, is your imagination. And then, having discovered, you start really to feed the sheep and you will stop, as of now, this walking of your Savior in the mud.

The Wish Fulfilled

Learn how to pray. Master it and make your world conform to the ideal you want to experience. Stop thinking of, and start thinking from. To think from the wish fulfilled is to realize that which you will never experience while you are thinking of it. When you put yourself into the state of the wish fulfilled and think from it, you are praying, and in a way your reasoning mind does not know, your wish will become a fact in your world. You can be the man or woman you want to be, when you know how to pray. All things are possible to him who believes, therefore learn the art of believing and persuade yourself it is true. Then one day, occupying space and time in your imagination, you will be seen by another, who will call or send you a letter verifying your visit. This I know from experience.

The Wish Fulfilled

When you pray you must immerse yourself in the feeling of the wish fulfilled, for the word "pray" means, "Motion towards; accession to; at or in the vicinity of." Point yourself towards the wish fulfilled and accept that invisible state as reality. Then go your way knowing the desire is now yours. You did it and you will not be surprised when it comes to pass.

When you first practice this technique you will be surprised when it happens; but when you learn how to completely accept the state assumed, you will know you do not have to do a thing to make it come to pass, as the assumption contains its own plan of fulfillment. You will know that this world is imaginal and that an assumption . . with no external object to support its truth . . will harden into fact when its truth is persisted in.

If an imaginal act produces an external fact to support it, then is not this world essentially imagined? If you dare to assume what your reason and senses deny and walk faithful to your assumption, believing in its reality . . and its corresponding effect is produced, can this seemingly solid, real world be anything other than imaginal? Everything is imagined, for you are God . . all imagination! God exists in you and you in Him. The world is all that you have imagined it to be, even though you cannot remember when or how you brought it into being.

The Wish Fulfilled

Let us take, for those who are here for the first time, truth on this level. A true judgment on this level must conform to the external facts to which it relates. If I should say now, "Isn't it a beautiful dog?" and you look, and there is no dog, my statement is a lie, for there is no dog to support my statement. That's a lie. But the Bible tells us that you can make the statement as I have just made it, and even though at the moment that you make it the senses deny it, you can assume that it is there, and persist in the assumption that it is, and in a way that no one knows, the dog will come there.

You can assume, "I AM rich," and not have a nickel in the bank; in fact, you don't have a bank account. You can assume, "I AM rich, and feel what it would be like if it were true. Now that assumption is a false statement if, at the moment of the assumption, your senses deny it and your reason denies it. So, that is false. Your Bible teaches that it is true if you persist in the assumption;

that the assumption, though false, if persisted in, will harden into fact. This is based upon the simple, simple statement that "Imagining creates reality;" that the true being called Jesus Christ is the human imagination. And all things are possible to Christ.

Well, can I imagine it? Yes. Can I believe it to be true? Well, try it. Can I persuade myself that the thing assumed is true? Well, assume it, and assume the feeling of the wish fulfilled. And my assumption, though at the moment of the assumption it is denied by my senses . . denied by my reason; if I persist in my assumption, it will harden into fact. That, I know from my own experience; that, I know from the experiences of hundreds of people who have written to me, and it has worked in their cases.

The Wish Fulfilled

If words come naturally, if I am asking some good for another, then I bring the other before my mind's eye and I tell him how thrilled I am because of his good fortune and try to persuade myself of the reality of that conversation, based upon what I would consider fact. For I look upon my imaginal act as fact. Before it becomes an objective fact, to me it just a fact . . it's a subjective fact which I have just appropriated prior to its becoming an objective fact. So, if words are natural at the time, I use words. But they are all internal. No one is going to hear them. God is not deaf and I don't have to scream at Him. You go to church, and all of a sudden the minister says, "Let us pray." Well, you can't do that in prayer. He's going to lead you in prayer! He is not what I want, and he starts to lead people, and your mind goes on constantly by his idle words. Now, that is not praying. When you pray, you are told, "Go within and close the door, and he who sees and hears in secret, he will reward you openly." Yet a minister dares to lead me in prayer! How can he lead me in prayer?

Let me go into the Silence by myself. They don't want the same things you want. When we went into the Silence . . how many there are here I don't know, but each had a different desire . . a different want in this world. How can I lead you in prayer? I do not know what you want, unless you tell me. But you yourself know what you would like. You may appropriate it. You feel yourself into the situation of the wish fulfilled. That's praying! I feel myself right into the state of the wish fulfilled, and then feel the naturalness of it. Give it all the tones of reality. Give it all the sensory vividness that you can muster. Then when I open my eyes, the world returns, and the world tells me that I am self-deceived. But I'll say to the world, Wait . . just wait a second, and we will see who is deceived.

And then when it happens, the world will always say, Well, it happened so naturally, it would have happened anyway. They always say that.

The Wish Fulfilled

You illuminate or darken your life by the ideas to which you consent. Nothing is more important to you than the ideas on which you feed. And you feed on the ideas from which you think. If you find the world unchanged, it is a sure sign that you are wanting in fidelity to the new mental diet, which you neglect in order to condemn your environment. You are in need of a new and sustained attitude.

You can be anything you please if you will make the conception habitual, for any idea which excludes all others from the field of attention discharges in action.

The ideas and moods to which you constantly return define the state with which you are fused. Therefore train yourself to occupy more frequently the feeling of your wish fulfilled. This is creative magic. It is the way to work toward fusion with the desired state.

If you would assume the feeling of your wish fulfilled more frequently, you would be master of your fate, but unfortunately you shut out your assumption for all but the occasional hour. Practice making real to yourself the feeling of the wish fulfilled.

After you have assumed the feeling of the wish fulfilled, do not close the experience as you would a book, but carry it around like a fragrant odor.

Instead of being completely forgotten, let it remain in the atmosphere communicating its influence automatically to your actions and reactions. A mood, often repeated, gains a momentum that is hard to break or check. So be careful of the feelings you entertain. Habitual moods reveal the state with which you are fused.

It is always possible to pass from thinking of the end you desire to realize, to thinking from the end.

But the crucial matter is thinking from the end, for thinking from means unification or fusion with the idea: whereas in thinking of the end, there is always subject and object . . the thinking individual and the thing thought.

You must imagine yourself into the state of your wish fulfilled, in your love for that state, and in so doing, live and think from it and no more of it. You pass from thinking of to thinking from by centering your imagination in the feeling of the wish fulfilled.

The Wish Fulfilled

Inner speech calls events into existence.

In every event, is the creative sound that is its life and being. All that a man believes and consents to as true reveals itself in his inner speech. It is his Word, his life.

Try to notice what you are saying in yourself at this moment, to what thoughts and feelings you are consenting. They will be perfectly woven into your tapestry of life.

To change your life, you must change your inner talking, for "life", said Hermes, "is the union of Word and Mind".

When imagination matches your inner speech to fulfilled desire, there will then be a straight path in yourself from within out, and the without will instantly reflect the within for you, and you will know reality is only actualized inner talking.

"Receive with meekness the inborn Word which is able to save your souls."

Every stage of man's progress is made by the conscious exercise of his imagination matching his inner speech to his fulfilled desire. Because man does not perfectly match them, the results are uncertain, while they might be perfectly certain.

Persistent assumption of the wish fulfilled is the means of fulfilling the intention.

As we control our inner talking, matching it to our fulfilled desires, we can lay aside all other processes. Then we simply act by clear imagination and intention. We imagine the wish fulfilled and carry on mental conversations from that premise.

Through controlled inner talking from premises of fulfilled desire, seeming miracles are performed.

The future becomes the present and reveals itself in our inner speech. To be held by the inner speech of fulfilled desire is to be safely anchored in life.

Our lives may seem to be broken by events, but they are never broken so long as we retain the inner speech of fulfilled desire. All happiness depends on the active voluntary use of imagination to construct and inwardly affirm that we are what we want to be.

We match ourselves to our ideals by constantly remembering our aim and identifying ourselves with it. We fuse with our aims by frequently occupying the feeling of our wish fulfilled. It is the frequency, the habitual occupancy, that is the secret of success. The oftener we do it, the more natural it is. Fancy assembles. Continuous imagination fuses.

The Wish Fulfilled

Fancy assembles, imagination fuses.

Here is a practical application of this theory.

A year ago, a blind girl living in the city of San Francisco found herself confronted with a transportation problem. A rerouting of buses forced her to make three transfers between her home and her office. This lengthened her trip from fifteen minutes to two hours and fifteen minutes. She thought seriously about this problem and came to the decision that a car was the solution. She knew that she could not drive a car but felt that she could be driven in one.

Putting this theory to the test that "whenever the actions of the inner self correspond to the actions which the outer, physical self must take to appease desire, that desire will be realized", she said to herself, "I will sit here and imagine that I am being driven to my office."

Sitting in her living room, she began to imagine herself seated in a car. She felt the rhythm of the motor. She imagined that she smelled the odor of gasoline, felt the motion of the car, touched the sleeve of the driver and felt that the driver was a man. She felt the car stop, and turning to her companion, said, "Thank you very much, sir."

To which he replied, "The pleasure is all mine."

Then she stepped from the car and heard the door snap shut as she closed it.

She told me that she centered her imagination on being in a car and, although blind, viewed the city from her imaginary ride. She did not think of the ride. She thought from the ride and all that it implied.

This controlled and subjectively directed purposive ride raised her imagination to its full potency. She kept her purpose ever before her, knowing there was cohesion in purposive inner movement. In these mental journeys, an emotional continuity must be sustained, the emotion of fulfilled desire. Expectancy and desire were so intensely joined that they passed at once from a mental state into a physical act.

The inner self moves along the predetermined course best when the emotions collaborate. The inner self must be fired, and it is best fired by the thought of great deeds and personal gain. We must take pleasure in our actions.

On two successive days, the blind girl took her imaginary ride, giving it all the joy and sensory vividness of reality. A few hours after her second imaginary ride, a friend told her of a story in the evening paper. It was a story of a man who was interested in the blind. The blind girl phoned him and stated her problem. The very next day, on his way home, he stopped in at a bar and while there had the urge to tell the story of the blind girl to his friend the proprietor. A total stranger, on hearing the story, volunteered to drive the blind girl home every day. The man who told the story then said, "If you will take her home, I will take her to work."

This was over a year ago, and since that day, this blind girl has been driven to and from her office by these two gentlemen.

Now, instead of spending two hours and fifteen minutes on three buses, she is at her office in less than fifteen minutes. And on that first ride to her office, she turned to her good Samaritan and said, "Thank you very much, sir"; and he replied, "The pleasure is all mine."

Thus, the objects of her imagination were to her the realities of which the physical manifestation was only the witness. The determinative animating principle was the imaginative ride. Her triumph could be a surprise only to those who did not know of her inner ride. She mentally viewed the world from this imaginative ride with such a clearness of vision that every aspect of the city attained identity.

These inner movements not only produce corresponding outer movements: this is the law which operates beneath all physical appearances. He who practices these exercises of bilocation will develop unusual powers of concentration and quiescence and will inevitably achieve waking consciousness on the inner and dimensionally larger world.

Actualizing strongly, she fulfilled her desire, for, viewing the city from the feeling of her wish fulfilled, she matched the state desired and granted that to herself which sleeping men ask of God.

To realize your desire, an action must start in your imagination, apart from the evidence of the senses, involving movement of self and implying fulfillment of your desire. Whenever it is the action which the outer self takes to appease desire, that desire will be realized.

The Wish Fulfilled

Lecture - Fundamentals . . 1953

From INTA Bulletin, "New Thought" summer 1953

WITH so vast a subject, it is indeed a difficult task to summarize in a few hundred words what I consider the

. . most basic ideas on which those who seek a true understanding of metaphysics should now concentrate. I shall do what I can in the shape of three fundamentals. These fundamentals are: Self-Observation, Definition of Aim, and Detachment.

The purpose of true metaphysics is to bring about a rebirth or radical psychological change in the individual. Such a change cannot take place until the individual first discovers the self that he would change. This discovery can be made only through an uncritical observation of his reactions to life. The sum total of these reactions defines the individual's state of consciousness, and it is the individual's state of consciousness that attracts the situations and circumstances of his life.

So the starting point of true metaphysics, on its practical side, is self-observation in order to discover one's reactions to life, reactions that form one's secret self . . the cause of the phenomena of life.

With Emerson, I accept the fact that "Man surrounds himself with the true image of himself . . . what we are, that only can we see."

There is a definite connection between what is outer and what is inner in man, and it is ever our inner states that attract our outer life. Therefore, the individual must always start with himself. It is one's self that must be changed.

Man, in his blindness, is quite satisfied with himself, but heartily dislikes the circumstances and situations of his life. He feels this way, not knowing that the cause of his displeasure lies not in the condition nor the person with whom he is displeased, but in the very self he likes so much. Not realizing that "he surrounds himself with the true image of himself" and that "what he is, that only can he see," he is shocked when he discovers that it has always been his own deceitfulness that made him suspicious of others.

Self-observation would reveal this deceitful one in all of us; and this one must be accepted before there can be any transformation of ourselves.

At this moment, try to notice your inner state. To what thoughts are you consenting? With what feelings are you identified? You must be ever careful where you are within yourself.

Most of its think that we are kind and loving, generous and tolerant, forgiving and noble; but an uncritical observation of our reactions to life will reveal a self that is not at all kind and loving, generous and tolerant, forgiving and noble. And it is this self that we must first accept and then set about to change.

Rebirth depends on inner work on one's self. No one can be reborn without changing this self. Any time that an entirely new set of reactions enters into a person's life, a change of consciousness has taken place, a spiritual rebirth has occurred.

Having discovered, through an uncritical observation of your reactions to life, a self that must be changed, you must now formulate an aim. That is, you must define the one you would like to be instead of the one you truly are in secret. With this aim clearly defined, you must, throughout your conscious waking day, notice your every reaction in regard to this aim.

The reason for this is that everyone lives in a definite state of consciousness, which state of consciousness we have already described as the sum total of his reactions to life. Therefore, in defining an aim, you are defining a state of consciousness, which, like all states of consciousness, must have its reactions to life. For example: if a rumor or an idle remark could cause an anxious reaction in one person and no reaction in another, this is positive proof that the two people are living in two different states of consciousness.

If you define your aim as a noble, generous, secure, kindly individual . . knowing that all things are states of consciousness . . you can easily tell whether you are faithful to your aim in life by watching your reactions to the daily events of life. If you are faithful to your ideal, your reactions will conform to your aim, for you will be identified with your aim and, therefore, will be thinking from your aim. If your reactions are not in harmony with your ideal, it is a sure sign that you are separated from your ideal and are only thinking of it. Assume that you are the loving one you want to be, and notice your reactions throughout the day in regard to that assumption; for your reactions will tell you the state from which you are operating.

This is where the third fundamental . . Detachment . . enters in. Having discovered that everything is a state consciousness made visible and having defined that particular state which we want to make visible, we now set about the task of entering such a state, for we must move psychologically from where we are to where we desire to be.

The purpose of practicing detachment is to separate us from our present reactions to life and attach us to our aim in life. This inner separation must be developed by practice. At first we seem to have no power to separate ourselves from undesirable inner states, simply because we have always taken every mood, every reaction, as natural and have become identified with them. When we have no idea that our reactions are only states of consciousness from which it is possible to separate ourselves, we go round and round in the same circle of problems . . not seeing them as inner states but as outer situations. We practice detachment, or inner separation, that we may escape from the circle of our habitual reactions to life. That is why we must formulate an aim and constantly notice ourselves in regard to that aim.

This teaching begins with self-observation. Secondly it asks, "What do you want?" And then it teaches detachment from all negative states and attachment to your aim. This last state. . attachment to your aim . . is accomplished by frequently assuming the feeling of your wish fulfilled.

We must practice separating ourselves from our negative moods and thoughts in the midst of all the troubles and disasters of daily life. No one can be different from what he is now unless he begins to separate himself from his present reactions and to identify himself with his aim. Detachment from negative states and assumption of the wish fulfilled must be practiced in the midst of all the blessings and cursing of life.

The way of true metaphysics lies in the midst of all that is going on in life. We must constantly practice self-observation, thinking from our aim, and detachment from negative moods and thoughts if we would be doers of truth instead of mere hearers.

Practice these three fundamentals and you will rise to higher and higher levels of consciousness. Remember, always, it is your state of consciousness that attracts your life.

The Wish Fulfilled

Lesson 2 from Neville's 1948 Classroom Lessons

Lesson 2

ASSUMPTIONS HARDEN INTO FACT

This Bible of ours has nothing to do with history.

Some of you may yet be inclined tonight to believe that, although we can give it a psychological interpretation, it still could be left in its present form and be interpreted literally.

You cannot do it.

The Bible has no reference at all to people or to events as you have been taught to believe. The sooner you begin to rub out that picture the better.

We are going to take a few stories tonight, and again I am going to remind you that you must reenact all of these stories within your own mind.

Bear in mind that although they seem to be stories of people fully awake, the drama is really between you, the sleeping one, the deeper you, and the conscious waking you.

They are personified as people, but when you come to the point of application you must remember the importance of the drowsy state.

All creation, as we told you last night, takes place in the state of sleep, or that state which is akin to sleep . . the, sleepy drowsy state.

We told you last night the first man is not yet awakened. You are Adam, the first man, still in the profound sleep.

The creative you is the fourth-dimensional you whose home is simply the state you enter when men call you asleep.

Our first story for tonight is found in the Gospel of John.

As you hear it unfold before you, I want you to compare it in your mind's eye to the story you heard last night from the book of Genesis.

The first book of the Bible, the book of Genesis, historians claim is the record of events which occurred on earth some 3,000 years before the events recorded in the book of John.

I ask you to be rational about it and see if you do not think the same writer could have written both stories. You be the judge as to whether the same inspired man could not have told the same story and told it differently.

This is a very familiar story, the story of the trial of Jesus. In this Gospel of John it is recorded that Jesus was brought before Pontius Pilate, and the crowd clamored for his life, they wanted Jesus.

Pilate turned to them and said:

"But ye have a custom, that I should release unto you one at the Passover; will ye therefore that I release unto you the King of the Jews? Then cried they all again, saying, Not this man, but Barabbas. Now Barabbas was a robber."

You are told that Pilate had no choice in the matter, he was only a judge interpreting law, and this was the law.

The people had to be given that which they requested. Pilate could not release Jesus against the wishes of the crowd, and so he released Barabbas and gave unto them Jesus to be crucified.

Now bear in mind that your consciousness is God. There is no other God. And you are told that God has a son whose name is Jesus.

If you will take the trouble to look up the word Barabbas in your concordance, you will see that it is a contraction of two Hebraic words: BAR, which means a daughter or son . . or child, and ABBA, which means father. Barabbas is the son of the great father. And Jesus in the story is called the Savior, the Son of the Father.

We have two sons in this story. And we have two sons in the story of Esau and Jacob.

Bear in mind that Isaac was blind, and justice to be true must be blind folded.

Although in this case Pilate is not physically blind, the part given to Pilate implies that he is blind because he is a judge. On all the great law buildings of the world we see the lady or the man who represents justice as being blindfolded.

"Judge not according to the appearance,
but judge righteous judgment.

Here we find Pilate is playing the same part as Isaac. There are two sons. All the characters as they appear in this story can apply to your own life. You have a son that is robbing you this very moment of that which you could be.

If you came to this meeting tonight conscious of wanting something, desiring something, you walked in the company of Barabbas.

For to desire is to confess that you do not now possess what you desire, and because all things are yours, you rob yourself by living in the state of desire.

My savior is my desire..

As I want something I am looking into the eyes of my savior.

But if I continue wanting it, I deny my Jesus, my savior, for as I want I confess I am not and

"except ye believe that I AM He ye die in your sins."

I cannot have and still continue to desire what I have. I may enjoy it, but I cannot continue wanting it.

Here is the story.

This is the feast of the Passover. Something is going to change right now, something is going to Passover. Man is incapable of passing over from one state of consciousness into another unless he releases from consciousness that which he now entertains, for it anchors him where he is.

You and I may go to physical feasts year after year as the sun enters the great sign of Aries, but it means nothing to the true mystical Passover.

To keep the feast of the Passover, the psychological feast, I pass from one state of consciousness into another.

I do it by releasing Barabbas, the thief and robber that robs me of that state which I could embody within my world.

The state I seek to embody is personified in the story as Jesus the Savior . If I become what I want to be then I am saved from what I was. If I do not become it, I continue to keep locked within me a thief who robs me of being that which I could be.

These stories have no reference to any persons who lived nor to any event that ever occurred upon earth. These characters are everlasting characters in the mind of every man in the world.

You and I perpetually keep alive either Barabbas or Jesus. You know at every moment of time who you are entertaining.

Do not condemn a crowd for clamoring that they should release Barabbas and crucify Jesus. It is not a crowd of people called Jews. They had nothing to do with it.

If we are wise, we too should clamor for the release of that state of mind that limits us from being what we want to be, that restricts us, that does not permit us to become the ideal that we seek and strive to attain in this world.

I am not saying that you are not tonight embodying Jesus. I only remind you, that if at this very moment you have an unfulfilled ambition, then you are entertaining that which denies the fulfillment of the ambition, and that which denies it is Barabbas.

To explain the mystical, psychological transformation known as the Passover, or the crossing over, you must now become identified with the ideal that you would serve, and you must remain faithful to the ideal.

If you remain faithful to it, you not only crucify it by your faithfulness, but you resurrect it unaided by a man.

As the story goes, no man could rise early enough to roll away the stone. Unaided by a man the stone was removed, and what seemingly was dead and buried was resurrected unassisted by a man.

You walk in the consciousness of being that which you want to be, no one sees it as yet, but you do not need a man to roll away the problems and the obstacles of life in order to express that which you are conscious of being.

That state has its own unique way of becoming embodied in this world, of becoming flesh that the whole world may touch it.

Now you can see the relationship between the story of Jesus and the story of Isaac and his two sons, where one transplanted the other, where one was called the Supplanter of the other.

Why do you think those who compiled the sixty odd books of our Bible made Jacob the forefather of Jesus?

They took Jacob, who was called the Supplanter, and made him father of twelve, then they took Judah or praise, the fifth son and made him the forefather of Joseph, who is supposed to have fathered in some strange way this one called Jesus.

Jesus must supplant Barabbas as Jacob must supplant and take the place of Esau.

Tonight you can sit right here and conduct the trial of your two sons, one of whom you want released.

You can become the crowd who clamors for the release of the thief, and the judge who willingly releases Barabbas, and sentences Jesus to fill his place.

He was crucified on Golgotha, the place of the skull, the seat of the imagination.

To experience the Passover or passage from the old to the new concept of self, you must release Barabbas, your present concept of self, which robs you of being that which you could be, and you must assume the new concept which you desire to express.

The best way to do this is to concentrate your attention upon the idea of identifying yourself with your ideal. Assume you are already that which you seek and your assumption, though false, if sustained, will harden into fact.

You will know when you have succeeded in releasing Barabbas, your old concept of self, and when you have successfully crucified Jesus, or fixed the new concept of self, by simply looking mentally at the people you know.

If you see them as you formerly saw them, you have not changed your concept of self, for all changes of concepts of self result in a changed relationship to your world.

We always seem to others an embodiment of the ideal we inspire. Therefore, in meditation, we must imagine that others see us as they would see us were we what we desire to be.

You can release Barabbas and crucify and resurrect Jesus if you will first define your ideal. Then relax in a comfortable arm chair, induce a state of consciousness akin to sleep and experience in imagination what you would experience in reality were you already that which you desire to be.

By this simple method of experiencing in imagination what you would experience in the flesh were you the embodiment of the ideal you serve, you release Barabbas who robbed you of your greatness, and you crucify and resurrect your savior, or the ideal you desired to express.

Now let us turn to the story of Jesus in the garden of Gethsemane. Bear in mind that a garden is a properly prepared plot of ground, it is not a wasteland.

You are preparing this ground called Gethsemane by coming here and studying and doing something about your mind. Spend some time daily in preparing your mind by reading good literature, listening to good music and entering into conversations that ennoble.

We are told in the Epistles,

"Whatsoever things are true, whatsoever things are honest, whatsoever things are just, whatsoever things are pure, whatsoever things are lovely, whatsoever

things are of good report; if there be any virtue, and if there be any praise, think on these things."

Continuing with our story, as told in the 18th chapter of John, Jesus is in the garden and suddenly a crowd begins to seek him. He is standing there in the dark and he says,

"Whom seek ye?"

The spokesman called Judas answers and says,

"We seek Jesus of Nazareth."

A voice answers,

"I AM He."

At this instant they all fall to the ground, thousands of them tumbled. That in itself should stop you right there and let you know it could not be a physical drama, because no one could be so bold in his claim that he is the one sought, that he could cause thousands who seek him to fall to the ground.

But the story tells us they all fell to the ground. Then when they regained their composure they asked the same question.

"Jesus answered, I have told you that I am He: if therefore ye seek me, let these go their way."

"Then said Jesus unto him, That thou doest, do quickly."

Judas, who has to do it quickly, goes out and commits suicide.

Now to the drama.

You are in your garden of Gethsemane or prepared mind. If you can, while you are in a state akin to sleep, control your attention and not let it wander away from its purpose. If you can do that you are definitely in the garden.

Very few people can sit quietly and not enter a reverie or a state of uncontrolled thinking.

When you can restrict the mental action and remain faithful to your watch, not permitting your attention to wander all over the place, but hold it without effort within a limited field of presentation to the state you are contemplating, then you are definitely this disciplined presence in the garden of Gethsemane.

The suicide of Judas is nothing more than changing your concept of yourself.

When you know what you want to be you have found your Jesus or savior.

When you assume that you are what you want to be you have died to your former concept of self (Judas committed suicide) and are now living as Jesus.

You can become at will detached from the world round about you, and attached to that which you want to embody within your world.

Now that you have found me, now that you have found that which would save you from what you are, let go of that which you are and all that it represents in the world. Become completely detached from it. In other words, go out and commit suicide.

You completely die to what you formerly expressed in this world, and you now completely live to that which no one saw as true of you before.

You are as though you had died by your own hand, as though you had committed suicide. You took your own life by becoming detached in consciousness from what you formerly kept alive, and you begin to live to that which you have discovered in your garden.

You have found your savior.

It is not men falling, not a man betraying another, but you detaching your attention, and refocusing your attention in an entirely new direction.

From this moment on you walk as though you were that which you formerly wanted to be.

Remaining faithful to your new concept of yourself you die or commit suicide. No one took your life, you laid it down yourself.

You must be able to see the relation of this to the death of Moses, where he so completely died that no one could find where he was buried. You must see the relationship of the death of Judas. He is not a man who betrayed a man called Jesus.

The word Judas is praise; it is Judah, to praise, to give thanks, to explode with joy.

You do not explode with joy unless you are identified with the ideal you seek and want to embody in this world. When you become identified with the state you contemplate you cannot suppress your joy. It rises like the fragrant odor described as Jericho in the Old Testament.

I am trying to show you that the ancients told the same story in all the stories of the Bible. All that they are trying to tell us is how to become that which we want to be. And they imply in every story that we do not need the assistance of another. You do not need another to become now what you really want to be.

Now we turn to a strange story in the Old Testament; one that very few priests and rabbis will be bold enough to mention from their pulpits.

Here is one who is going to receive the promise as you now receive it. His name is Jesus, only the ancients called him Joshua, Jehoshua Ben Nun, or savior, son of the fish, the Savior of the great deep.

Nun means fish, and fish is the element of the deep, the profound ocean. Jehoshua means Jehovah saves, and Ben means the offspring or son of. So he was called the one who brought the fish age.

This story is in the 6th book of the Bible, the book of Joshua. A promise is made to Joshua as it is made to Jesus in the Anglicized form in the gospels of Matthew, Mark, Luke and John.

In the gospel of John, Jesus says,

"All things whatsoever thou hast given me are of thee."

"And all mine are thine, and thine are mine."

In the Old Testament in the book of Joshua it is said in these words:

"Every place that the sole of your foot shall tread upon, that have I given unto you."

It does not matter where it is; analyze the promise and see if you can accept it literally. It is not physically true but it is psychologically true. Wherever you can stand in this world mentally that you can realize.

Joshua is haunted by this promise that wherever he can place his foot (the foot is understanding), wherever the sole of his foot shall tread, that will be given unto him. He wants the most desirable state in the world, the fragrant city, the delightful state called Jericho.

He finds himself barred by the impassable walls of Jericho. He is on the outside, as you are now on the outside.

You are functioning three-dimensionally and you cannot seem to reach the fourth-dimensional world where your present desire is already a concrete objective reality. You cannot seem to reach it because your senses bar you from it. Reason tells you it is impossible, all things round about you tell you it is not true.

Now you employ the services of a harlot and a spy, and her name is Rahab.

The word Rahab simply means the spirit of the father. RACE means the breath or spirit, and AB the father. Hence we find that this harlot is the spirit of the father and the father is man's awareness of being aware, man's I AMness, man's consciousness.

Your capacity to feel is the great spirit of the father, and that capacity is Rahab in this story. She has two professions that of a spy and that of a harlot.

The profession of a spy is this: to travel secretly, to travel so quietly that you may not be detected. There is not a single physical spy in this world who can travel so quietly that he will be altogether unseen by others. He may be very wise in concealing his ways, and he may never be truly apprehended, but at every moment of time he runs the risk of being detected.

When you are sitting quietly with your thoughts, there is no man in the world so wise that he can look at you and tell you where you are mentally dwelling.

I can stand here and place myself in London. Knowing London quite well, I can close my eyes and assume that I am actually standing in London.

If I remain within this state long enough, I will be able to surround myself with the environment of London as though it were a solid concrete objective fact.

Physically I am still here, but mentally I am thousands of miles away and I have made elsewhere here. I do not go there as a spy, I mentally make elsewhere here, and then now.

You cannot see me dwelling there, so you think I have just gone to sleep and that I am still here in this world, this three-dimensional world that is now San Francisco. As far as I am physically concerned, I am here but no one can tell me where I am when I enter the moment of meditation.

Rahab's next profession was that of a harlot, which is to grant unto men what they ask of her without asking man's right to ask. If she be an absolute harlot, as her name implies, then she possesses all and can grant all that man asks of her. She is there to serve, and not to question man's right to seek what he seeks of her.

You have within you the capacity to appropriate a state without knowing the means that will be employed to realize that end and you assume the feeling of the wish fulfilled without having any of the talents that men claim you must possess in order to do so.

When you appropriate it in consciousness you have employed the spy, and because you can embody that state within yourself by actually giving it to yourself, you are the harlot, for the harlot satisfies the man who seeks her.

You can satisfy self by appropriating the feeling that you are what you want to be. And this assumption though false, that is, although reason and the senses deny it, if persisted in will harden into fact. By actually embodying that which you have assumed you are, you have the capacity to become completely satisfied.

Unless it becomes a tangible, concrete reality you will not be satisfied; you will be frustrated.

You are told in this story that when Rahab went into the city to conquer it, the command given to her was to enter the heart of the city, the heart of the matter, the very center of it, and there remain until I come.

Do not go from house to house, do not leave the upper room of the house into which you enter. If you leave the house and there be blood upon your head, it is upon your head. But if you do not leave the house and there be blood, it shall be upon my head.

Rahab goes into the house, rises to the upper floor, and there she remains while the walls crumble.

That is, we must keep a high mood if we would walk with the highest. In a very veiled manner, the story tells you that when the walls crumbled and Joshua entered, the only one who was saved in the city was the spy and the harlot whose name was Rahab.

This story tells what you can do in this world. You will never lose the capacity to place yourself elsewhere and make it here. You will never lose the ability to give unto yourself what you are bold enough to appropriate as true of self. It has nothing to do with the woman who played that part.

The explanation of the crumbling of the walls is simple.

You are told that he blew upon the trumpet seven times and at the seventh blast the walls crumbled and he entered victoriously into the state that he sought.

Seven is a stillness, a rest, the Sabbath. It is the state when man is completely unmoved in his conviction that the thing is. When I can assume the feeling of my wish fulfilled and go to sleep, unconcerned, undisturbed, I am at rest mentally, and am keeping the Sabbath or am blowing the trumpet seven times.

And when I reach that point the walls crumble. Circumstances alter then remold themselves in harmony with my assumption. As they crumble I resurrect that which I have appropriated within. The walls, the obstacles, the problems, crumble of their own weight if I can reach the point of stillness within me.

The man Who can fix within his own mind's eye an idea, even though the world would deny it, if he remains faithful to that idea he will see it manifested.

There is all the difference in the world between holding the idea, and being held by the idea. Become so dominated by an idea that it haunts the mind as though you were it. Then, regardless of what others may say, you are walking in the direction of your fixed attitude of mind. You are walking in the direction of the idea that dominates the mind.

As we told you last night, you have but one gift that is truly yours to give, and that is yourself. There is no other gift; you must press it out of yourself by an appropriation.

It is there within you now for creation is finished. There is nothing to be that is not now. There is nothing to be created for all things are already yours, they are all finished.

Although man may not be able to stand physically upon a state, he can always stand mentally upon any desired state. By standing mentally I mean that you can now, this very moment, close your eyes and visualize a place other than your present one, and assume that you are actually there. You can feel this to be so real that upon opening your eyes you are amazed to find that you are not physically there.

This mental journey into the desired state, with its subsequent feeling of reality, is all that is necessary to bring about its fulfillment.

Your dimensionally greater Self has ways that the lesser, or three-dimensional you, know not of.

Furthermore, to the greater you, all means are good which promote the fulfillment of your assumption.

Remain in the mental state defined as your objective until it has the feeling of reality , and all the forces of heaven and earth will rush to aid its embodiment.

Your greater Self will influence the actions and words of all who can be used to aid the production of your fixed mental attitude.

Now we turn to the book of Numbers and here we find a strange story. I trust that some of you have had this experience as described in the bock of Numbers. They speak of the building of a tabernacle at the command of God; that God commanded Israel to build him a place of worship.

He gave them all the specifications of the tabernacle. It had to be an elongated, movable place of worship, and it had to be covered with skin. Need you be told anything more? Isn't that man?

"Know ye not that ye are the temple of God,
and that the Spirit of God dwelleth in you?"

There is no other temple. Not a temple made with hands, but a temple eternal in the heavens. This temple is elongated, and it is covered with skin, and it moves across the desert.

"And on the day that the tabernacle was reared up the cloud covered the tabernacle, namely, the tent of the testimony: and at even there was upon the tabernacle as it were the appearance of fire, until the morning. So it was always: the cloud covered it by day, and the appearance of fire by night."

The command given to Israel was to tarry until the cloud ascended by day and the fire by night.

"Whether it were two days, or a month, or a year, that the cloud tarried upon the tabernacle, remaining thereon, the children of Israel abode in their tents, and journeyed not: but when it was taken up, they journeyed."

You know that you are the tabernacle, but you may wonder, what is the cloud. In meditation many of you must have seen it. In meditation, this cloud, like the sub-soil waters of an artesian well, springs spontaneously to your head and forms itself into pulsating, golden rings. Then, like a gentle river they flow from your head in a stream of living rings of gold.

In a meditative mood bordering on sleep the cloud ascends. It is in this drowsy state that you should assume that you are that which you desire to be, and that you have that which you seek, for the cloud will assume the form of your assumption and fashion a world in harmony with itself.

The cloud is simply the garment of your consciousness, and where your consciousness is placed, there you will be in the flesh also.

This golden cloud comes in meditation. There is a certain point when you are approaching sleep that it is very, very thick, very liquid, and very much alive and pulsing. It begins to ascend as you reach the drowsy, meditative state, bordering on sleep. You do not strike the tabernacle; neither do you move it until the cloud begins to ascend.

The cloud always ascends when man approaches the drowsiness of sleep. For when a man goes to sleep, whether he knows it or not, he slips from a three-dimensional world into a fourth-dimensional world and that which is ascending is the consciousness of that man in a greater focus; it is a fourth-dimensional focus. What you now see ascending is your greater self. When that begins to ascend you enter into the actual state of feeling you are what you want to be. That is the time you lull yourself into the mood of being what you want to be, by either experiencing in imagination what you would experience in reality were you already that which you want to be, or by repeating over and over again the phrase that implies you have already done what you want to do.

A phrase such as, "Isn't it wonderful, isn't it wonderful," as though some wonderful thing had happened to you.

"In a dream, in a vision of the night,
when deep sleep falleth upon men,
in slumberings upon the bed.
Then he openeth the ears of men,
and sealeth their instruction."

Use wisely the interval preceding sleep.

Assume the feeling of the wish fulfilled and go to sleep in this mood.

At night, in a dimensionally larger world, when deep sleep falleth upon men, they see and play the parts that they will later on play on earth.

And the drama is always in harmony with that which their dimensionally greater selves read and play through them. Our illusion of free will is but ignorance of the causes which make us act.

The sensation which dominates the mind of man as he falls asleep, though false, will harden into fact.

Assuming the feeling of the wish fulfilled as we fall asleep, is the command to this embodying process saying to our mood,

"Be thou actual."

In this way we become through a natural process what we desire to be.

I can tell you dozens of personal experiences where it seemed impossible to go elsewhere, but by placing myself elsewhere mentally as I was about to go to sleep, circumstances changed quickly which compelled me to make the journey.

I have done it across water by placing myself at night on my bed as though I slept where I wanted to be. As the days unfolded things began to mold themselves in harmony with that assumption and all things that must happen to compel my journey did happen. And I, in spite of myself, must make ready to go toward that place which I assumed I was in when I approached the deep of sleep.

As my cloud ascends I assume that I am now the man I want to be, or that I am already in the place where I want to visit. I sleep in that place now. Then life strikes the tabernacle, strikes my environment and reassembles my environment across seas or over land and reassembles it in the likeness of my assumption. It has nothing to do with men walking across a physical desert.

The whole vast world round about you is a desert.

From the cradle to the grave you and I walk as though we walk the desert.

But we have a living tabernacle wherein God dwells, and it is covered with a cloud which can and does ascend when we go to sleep or are in a state akin to sleep. Not necessarily in two days, it can ascend in two minutes. Why did they give you two days? If I now become the man I want to be, I may become dissatisfied tomorrow. I should at least give it a day before I decide to move on.

The Bible says in two days, a month, or a year: whenever you decide to move on with this tabernacle let the cloud ascend. As it ascends you start moving where the cloud is.

The cloud is simply the garment of your consciousness, your assumption.

Where the consciousness is placed you do not have to take the physical body; it gravitates there in spite of you.

Things happen to compel you to move in the direction where you are consciously dwelling.

"In my Father's house are many mansions: if it were not so, I would have told you. I go to prepare a place for you. And if I go and prepare a place for you, I will come again, and receive you unto myself; that where I AM, there ye may be also."

The many mansions are the unnumbered states within your mind, for you are the house of God.

In my Father's house are unnumbered concepts of self.

You could not in eternity exhaust what you are capable of being.

If I sit quietly here and assume that I am elsewhere, I have gone and prepared a place.

But if I open my eyes, the bilocation which I created vanishes and I am back here in the physical form that I left behind me as I went to prepare a place. But I prepared the place nevertheless and will in time dwell there physically.

You do not have to concern yourself with the ways and the means that will be employed to move you across space into that place where you have gone and mentally prepared it. Simply sit quietly, no matter where you are, and mentally actualize it.

But I give you warning, do not treat it lightly, for I am conscious of what it will do to people who treat it lightly. I treated it lightly once because I just wanted to get away, based only upon the temperature of the day.

It was in the deep of winter in New York, and I so desired to be in the warm climate of the Indies, that I slept that night as though I slept under palm trees. Next morning when I awoke it was still very much winter.

I had no intentions of going to the Indies that year, but distressing news came which compelled me to make the journey. It was in the midst of war when ships were being sunk right and left, but I sailed out of New York on a ship 48 hours after I received this news. It was the only way I could get to Barbados, and I arrived just in time to see my mother and say a three-dimensional "Good-bye" to her .

In spite of the fact that I had no intentions of going, the deeper Self watched where the great cloud descended. I placed it in Barbados and this tabernacle (my body) had to go and make the journey to fulfill the command,

"Wherever the sole of your foot shall tread
that have I given unto you."

Wherever the cloud descends in the desert, there you reassemble that tabernacle.

I sailed from New York at midnight on a ship without taking thought of submarines or anything else. I had to go. Things happened in a way that I could not have devised.

I warn you, do not treat it lightly. Do not say, "I will experiment and put myself in Labrador, just to see if it will work." You will go to your Labrador and then you will wonder why you ever came to this class. It will work if you dare assume the feeling of your wish fulfilled as you go to sleep.

Control your moods as you go to sleep.

I cannot find any better way to describe this technique than to call it a "controlled waking dream."

In a dream you lose control, but try preceding your sleep with a complete controlled waking dream, entering into it as you do in dream, for in a dream you are always very dominant, you always play the part.

You are always an actor in a dream, and never the audience. When you have a controlled waking dream you are an actor and you enter into the act of the controlled dream. But do not do it lightly, for you must then reenact it physically in a three-dimensional world.

Now before we go into our moment of silence there is something I must make very clear, and that is this effort we discussed last night.

If there is one reason in this whole vast world why people fail it is because they are unaware of a law known to psychologists today as the law of reverse effort.

When you assume the feeling of your wish fulfilled it is with a minimum of effort. You must control the direction of the movements of your attention. But you must do it with the least effort. If there is effort in the control, and you are compelling it in a certain way you are not going to get the results. You will get the opposite results, whatever they might be.

That is why we insist on establishing the basis of the Bible as Adam slept. That is the first creative act, and there is no record where he was ever awakened from this profound sleep. While he sleeps creation stops.

You change your future best when you are in control of your thoughts while in a state akin to sleep, for then effort is reduced to its minimum.

Your attention seems to completely relax, and then you must practice holding your attention within that feeling, without using force, and without using effort.

Do not think for a moment that it is will power that does it.

When you release Barabbas and become identified with Jesus, you do not will yourself to be it, you imagine that you are it. That is all you do.

Now as we come to the vital part of the evening, the interval devoted to prayer, let me again clarify the technique.

Know what you want. Then construct a single event, an event which implies fulfillment of your wish. Restrict the event to a single act.

For instance, if I single out as an event, shaking a man's hand, then that is the only thing I do. I do not shake it, then light a cigarette and do a thousand other things. I simply imagine that I am actually shaking hands and keep the act going over and over and over again until the imaginary act has all the feeling of reality.

The event must always imply fulfillment of the wish.

Always construct an event which you believe you would naturally encounter following the fulfillment of your desire.

You are the judge of what event you really want to realize.

There is another technique I gave you last night. If you cannot concentrate on an act, if you cannot snuggle into your chair and believe the chair is elsewhere, just as though elsewhere were here, then do this:

Reduce the idea, condense it to a single, simple phrase like, "Isn't it wonderful." or, "Thank you." or, "It's done." or, "It's finished."

There should not be more than three words.

Something that implies the desire is already realized. "Isn't it wonderful", or "Thank you," certainly imply that.

These are not all the phrases you could use. Make up out of your own vocabulary the phrase which best suits you. But make it very, very short and always use a phrase that implies fulfillment of the idea.

When you have your phrase in mind, lift the cloud. Let the cloud ascend by simply inducing the state that borders on sleep. Simply begin to imagine and feel you are sleepy, and in this state assume the feeling of the wish fulfilled.

Then repeat the phrase over and over like a lullaby. Whatever the phrase is, let it imply that the assumption is true, that it is concrete, that it is already a fact and you know it.

Just relax and enter into the feeling of actually being what you want to be. As you do it you are entering Jericho with your spy who has the power to give it. You are releasing Barabbas and sentencing Jesus to be crucified and resurrected. All these stories you are re-enacting if now you begin to let go and enter into the feeling of actually being what you want to be. Now we can go.....

Silence Period

Metaphysical / Law of Attraction Books

Neville Goddard's Interpretation of Scripture: Unlocking The Secrets of The Bible (2018)

The Neville Goddard Collection (All 10 of his books plus 2 Lecture series) (2016)

Neville Goddard - Consciousness: The Giver of All Gifts (2019)

Neville Goddard - Assumptions Harden Into Facts: The Book (2016)

Neville Goddard - Imagination: The Redemptive Power in Man (2016)

Neville Goddard - The World is At Your Command - The Very Best of Neville Goddard (2017)

Neville Goddard - Imagining Creates Reality - 365 Mystical Daily Quotes (2017)

Neville Goddard - Your Inner Conversations Are Creating Your World (2015)

David Allen - The Power of I AM (2014), The Power of I AM - Volume 2 (2015) , The Power of I AM - Volume 3 (2017)

David Allen - The Creative Power of Thought, Man's Greatest Discovery (2017) (compilation)

David Allen - The Secrets, Mysteries & Powers of The Subconscious Mind (2017) (compilation)

David Allen - The Money Bible - The Secrets of Attracting Prosperity (2017) (compilation)

David Allen - Your Faith Is Your Fortune, Your Unlimited Power (2018) (compilation)

David Allen - ASKffirmations: Questions That Create Reality (2018)

David Allen - The Within Creates The Without: Creating Our Lives By Design: Daily Meditations

David Allen - The Creative Power Of Mind: Daily Meditations For A Better Life

The Definitive Christian D. Larson Collection (6 Volumes, 30 books) (2014)

Fulfill All Your Desires With The Simple Act of Believing That They Are Already Fulfilled.

CPSIA information can be obtained
at www.ICGtesting.com
Printed in the USA
JSHW020859120123
36147JS00003BA/622

9 780999 543597